Today
Then

Today
Then

America's Best Minds
Look 100 Years into the Future
on the Occasion of the 1893
World's Columbian Exposition

Compiled & Introduced by

Dave Walter

American & World Geographic Publishing

Library of Congress Cataloging-in-Publication Data

Today then : America's best minds look 100 years into the future on the occasion of the 1893 World's Columbian Exposition / compiled & introduced by Dave Walter.

    p.   cm.

Includes index.

ISBN 1-56037-024-6

1. Twentieth century--Forecasts. 2. United States--Social life and customs--1865-1918. 3. Forecasting--History--19th century. 4. World's Columbian Exposition (1893 : Chicago, Ill.) I. Walter, Dave, date.

CB161.T56 1992

303.49'09'05--dc20   92-35385

Portraits (except those on pages 72, 90, 118, 130, 197 and 202) are reprinted from *Dictionary of American Portraits* (New York: 1967) through the courtesy of Dover Publications, Inc. Building illustrations are architect's sketches from *Portfolio: World's Columbian Exposition 1893* (Chicago: Winters Art Lithography Company, 1891).

Printed in the United States of America

To my parents, Dorothy and George Walter—

who taught me that looking back
was every bit as important
as looking forward

Contents

ADMINISTRATION BUILDING.

Preface

My greatest debt for this work is to Ms. Barbara Fifer, the senior editor for American & World Geographic Publishing. For she introduced me to this contortionist's view of the 1990s, found while she was scanning Montana newspapers from the early 1890s. Barb has performed on this manuscript (as she did on my manuscript for *Christmastime in Montana* in 1990) a judicious, perceptive, thoughtful, and effective editing. Her suggestions are unerringly helpful, her organization enhances the material, and her ability never to forget the reader and his perspective makes her a remarkable editor and friend.

The task of assembling background information on the American Press Association and the World's Columbian Exposition could not have been accomplished without the excellent assistance of Ms. Becky Lang, an honors student in journalism at Northwestern University in Evanston. Despite all of her academic responsibilities, Becky found research time for this project, and I am most grateful for her help.

For assistance, advice, and material, I am indebted to Mr. Harold P. Pluimer, an educational futurist in great demand nationally as a platform speaker on this topic. Mr. Pluimer's willingness to dip a drylander in the river of futurism—while neither frightening nor drowning him—can only be considered an act of faith.

As popular as were these 74 writers in 1892, some of their trails have dimmed with time. Only with the selfless assistance of a cadre of librarians, archivists, and researchers across the country could I have compiled sufficient biographical information to write the introductory sketches.

Among the most gracious of these professionals are: Ms. Nancy Blankenhorn, Reference Assistant at the New Jersey Historical Society in Newark; Mr. James Bradley, Research Assistant at the New York Stock Exchange in New York City; Ms. Emily Clark, Assistant Librarian at the Chicago Historical Society in Chicago; Professor H. D. Hampton of the History Department, University of Montana in Missoula; Mr. Richard Harms, Archivist in the Michigan Room of the Grand Rapids Public Library.

Of equal indispensability were: Mr. Fred W. Hunter, Information Manager for the American Medical Association in Chicago; Mr. Hinkle McLendon, Jr., a private researcher in Charleston, South Carolina; Ms. Eileen J. O'Brien, Special Collections Librarian at the New York State Historical Association in

Cooperstown; Ms. Susan Richardson, Archivist for the Historical Society of the Town of Greenwich, Connecticut; Ms. Anne Rosebrock, Librarian at the South Carolina Historical Society in Charleston; Ms. Laurie Thompson, a contract researcher in New York City; Ms. Marge Topps, a private researcher associated with the Chicago Genealogical Society; the reference staff in the Library-Archives Division of the Ohio Historical Society in Columbus.

In addition, several persons deserve special recognition for their assistance. At various points in this project—when problems threatened to kill the monster—they provided essential information, advice, and encouragement, and they breathed life back into the beast. My sincerest gratitude to: Ms. Mary Carey, Reference Librarian at The New-York Historical Society; Professor Bill Evans of the Department of History at the University of Montana in Missoula; Ms. Kathryn M. Harris, Supervisor of Reference/Technical Services at the Illinois Historical Library in Springfield.

No manuscript is researched and developed without the countless sacrifices of an author's family. Thus it should not be surprising that my teenage daughters, Emily and Amanda, have been quick to remind me that they have suffered grievous social and psychological deprivation as a direct result of a reduction in that buzz-concept "quality time." Only fools attempt to persuade teenagers with truth, so: To Emily and Amanda, I apologize. I am solely responsible for whatever psychological tics either one might develop as a result of my work on this manuscript, ever.

To my wife, Marcella, falls my greatest personal obligation. She remains my toughest—and, therefore, my most valuable—critic. She sees patterns and developments as I never will, and she can make cohesive what to me is disparate. She sacrifices plans and time and activities so I might write, and then she shares the drudge-work involved in manuscript preparation. For judgment and perspective on which I can rely, I am especially indebted to her. Again, thank you, dear.

Introduction

"By the 1990s, longevity will be so improved that 150 years will be no unusual age to reach."

Thomas De Witt Talmage

"Men will navigate the air, and smoke will be suppressed."

W. A. Peffer

"In the 1990s, the United States will be a government of perhaps 60 states, situated in both North and South America."

Asa C. Matthews

"Woman shall have the sole right to say when she shall wear the crown of motherhood."

Mary E. Lease

"By the end of the Twentieth Century, taxation will be reduced to a minimum, the entire world will be open to trade, and there will be no need of a standing army."

Erastus Wiman

"Each reasonably well-to-do man (and there will be lots of them in the 1990s) will have a telephote [sic] in his residence. By means of this device, the entertainment of any place of amusement in that city may be seen as well as heard."

Octavus Cohen

Today Then presents 74 pieces written in the early 1890s by noted commentators on the American scene. The American Press Association, a ready-print syndicate based in New York City, originally commissioned the writings. The A.P.A. ran this series in weekly newspapers across the country as a prelude to the opening of the World's Columbian Exposition in Chicago on May 1, 1893. That Chicago fair remains one of the most amazing events in an amazing decade—an American socio-cultural landmark.

Most of these writers become futurists, because they attempt to predict aspects of American society 100 years hence—in the 1990s. In the process, they produce insights into American life *both* in the 1890s and in the 1990s. They also encounter the various difficulties inherent in such predictions.

As an introduction to these 74 selections, this essay describes the nature of the United States in the early 1890s, the Chicago world's fair, and the American Press Association as a newspaper phenomenon. It also introduces the field of futurism—with which all Americans will deal in the 1990s, as the Twentieth Century is concluded and a new millennium begins. Thus the games with time continue: *Today Then.*

The United States of the early 1890s exhibited all of the strengths, all of the promises, and all of the problems of a young nation. It had bumped and stumbled through childhood and adolescence. With no little luck, it emerged in the last decade of the Nineteenth Century a virile, exuberant country of immense potential—but a nation caught in paradox.

Certainly the U.S. remained in the shadow of its European parents in international relations and the arts. Yet it had settled North America from the Atlantic to the Pacific, and it was beginning to look both north and south. Manifest Destiny was proving a difficult mistress to deny, once fully embraced.

The United States exhibited the problems of a nation in transition. It had spent the preceding century spreading across the continent and avoiding foreign entanglements. It was not an international power, with all of the concomitant privileges and responsibilities. Not until the Spanish-American War (1898-1899) would its heartfelt belief in Manifest Destiny stretch overseas.

In the early 1890s, the United States still focused on the Western Hemisphere. This nation recently had concluded its last major Indian war with the capture of Geronimo (1886) and had quelled the final Native American resistance at Wounded Knee (1890). This country just had created Yosemite and Sequoia national parks. Its focus remained domestic. In fact, this nation continued to work mightily to emerge from the shadow of the Civil War, concluded fewer than 30 years earlier.

In 1890 also, the U.S. Superintendent of the Census declared that a discernible frontier no longer existed in the western United States. Frederick Jackson Turner keyed (1893) his thesis of the American West on this declaration—a signal that an era had ended. From a country of 3.9 million in 1790, the U.S. had grown to 31.4 million by 1860, and then doubled its population to 62.6 million in 1890. If an era had ended, the nation's population boom had not.

On a map, the United States of the early 1890s appears well-formed. The current Union was short only six states: Utah (1896); Oklahoma (1907); New Mexico (1912); Arizona (1912); Alaska (1959); Hawaii (1959). Yet life within that Union differed significantly from today. For example, citizens in the early

1890s were not protected by (or subjected to) a series of subsequent Constitutional amendments. These range from a federal income tax to national prohibition and from the vote for women and 18-year-olds to refinements in Presidential tenure.

In the early 1890s, Americans relied primarily on newspapers and magazines for popular communication, with expanding postal and telegraphic systems. They witnessed the evolution of distinctly American architecture in the construction of the first true skyscraper, the Wainwright Building in St. Louis, and in the use of functional form, as in the Monadnock Building in Chicago. Yet the field of medicine remained relatively primitive. Scientists concentrated on developing antitoxins to immunize the population against pandemic diseases; doctors merely experimented with serious operations such as appendectomies and open-heart surgery.

In an age that relied almost exclusively on horse and "iron horse" transportation, other forms of travel burgeoned. Hot-air balloon, dirigible, and glider flight presaged air transportation. The "big wheel" bicycle quickly gave way to the "safety bike" model. Early forms of gasoline-driven motor vehicles appeared as curiosities. And the application of that remarkable discovery—electricity—to carriage transport had spawned electric trolley lines in more than 200 U.S. cities by 1890. If technology were not a goddess, at least she had become a princess with aspirations.

Expansion, growth, opportunity, development—all became elements of America's preoccupation with *progress*. As Charles Darwin and Herbert Spencer preached the doctrines of competition and natural selection in the face of fundamentalist religion, evolution justified America's mission even more conclusively. In this scheme, the role of the federal government, of any government, remained *laissez faire*.

Bigger *was* better! Technology *would* provide answers to pressing problems before social devastation resulted. In 1891 the New York Central's *Empire State Express* travelled the 436 miles from New York City to East Buffalo in a record-breaking 7 hours and 6 minutes. Improvements in car suspension, track construction, and motive power improved on that speed almost immediately. Corporations would develop these improvements—and if not corporations, then syndicates and conglomerates. Bigger *was* better.

Yet America in the early 1890s was trapped in paradox. Its society, for example, lacked order. For all of the promise inherent in the Industrial Revolution—technological discoveries, sprawling factories, ever-increasing production, radical inventions, *progress*—Americans flirted dangerously with social chaos. So great the immigration, so quick the commercial expansion, so rapid the disparity of classes, so significant the challenges to an agrarian heritage: often the social fabric seemed weakly woven, prone to unravel.

Marked fluctuations in the national economy drove much of the Victorian Age in the United States. After a severe crash in 1873, the country dropped into a long-wave depression—punctuated by business upswings in 1878, 1885, and 1892. Nevertheless, the withdrawal of foreign investment capital and apprehension over a stable monetary policy precipitated the severe Panic of 1893. Before the end of that year, 491 banks and more than 15,000 commercial institutions had failed. And that depression extended into 1897.

This unstable economic situation directly affected American society. Labor organizations flourished and strikes plagued many industries. Such violent clashes between strikers and authorities as the Haymarket Square Massacre (1886) in Chicago and the Homestead Steel Strike of 1892 reflect the extent of these labor-management divisions.

In response to this sentiment, third-party movements gained widespread support. The most significant became the agrarian/reform Populist Party, which proved an important factor in the national election of 1892. More lasting reform developed with Congressional action on child labor, interstate commerce, and pure food and drugs. And private social-reform efforts like Jane Addams' opening of Hull House in Chicago marked a popular social conscience. Still, some observers commented that the national fabric appeared to be fraying and might be on the verge of unraveling.

The most apparent effects of the country's severe economic fluctuations could be seen in the lives of its diverse peoples. Massive annual immigrations—particularly the "New Immigration" from central and southern Europe after 1885—rendered American society in the 1890s devastatingly ethnocentric. The disparity between the upper, white, capitalist class and the lower, also overwhelmingly white, laboring class was both apparent and remarkable. The possibility of social revolution loomed over America.

In an age that built the "grand hotels" in American cities, most citizens could aspire merely to day labor in these magnificent urban oases. Since this society sported only a minor middle class, the contrast between the American elite and the masses remained stark. Andrew Carnegie's *noblesse oblige* "Gospel of Wealth" merely punctuated these class cleavages.

Some aspects of popular American society from this era remain quite recognizable: Johnson and Johnson Pharmaceuticals; Coca-Cola; Sears, Roebuck, and Company; Maxwell House Coffee; Log Cabin Syrup; the Kodak camera. Other features—like "Jim Crow" legislation, enforcing racial segregation—prove more representative of that time. The "feel" of the time remains recognizable today, but the imprints of intervening technology and social reform skew our view of the milieu.

Despite the many paradoxes, however, the early 1890s in the United States offered a time of excitement and surprise. Whether called the Gilded Age, the *Belle Epoque*, the Industrial Age, the Mauve Decade, or the Victorian Era, this era provided involvement in a great national adventure, a national experience tied to technology and wealth and expansion.

American *progress* might have been divinely ordained, but it also was fraught with risk. America might have been on an expansive building spree, but it also failed to offer opportunity for all of its citizens. And all of these social strengths and weaknesses became evident in that era's greatest show: the World's Columbian Exposition, held in Chicago in 1893.

As the national economy began to disintegrate in 1892, World's Fair organizers—with Congressional backing—commemorated the four-hundredth anniversary of the landing of Christopher Columbus in the Western Hemisphere with the public dedication of the fair park in Chicago. Simultaneous with the Crash of 1893, the World's Columbian Exposition played to more than 27 million fairgoers during a six-month period—and touched the lives of practically every American. It became the most famous fair ever conducted on American soil.

On the basis of the Centennial Exposition, held in Philadelphia in 1876, organizers of the Chicago fair planned to show Americans just where they stood in relation to other cultures, just what tools were available for advancement, and just what the future might hold.

Given the age, the Exposition's theme was obvious: the national progress of the United States. Yet this world's fair would do more than just document the present and provide working models of the future. It would demonstrate the unity of America and hint that further progress and development would result in an eventual utopian condition. The fair contributed significantly to urban planning, to beaux-arts architecture, to distinctly American arts, and to the popularization of technology. It keyed its presentations on electricity, which promised unlimited power for the new century.

Once Jackson Park, on Chicago's South Side, had been drained and transformed into a temporary kingdom, it became a symbol of the nation's cohesion, self-confidence, and triumphant *progress*—all in the face of a massive national economic disaster. The formal portion of the grounds included huge structures of architectural wonder, organized by subject: Machinery, Agriculture, Transportation, Liberal Arts, Electricity, etc.

These central buildings were constructed of a relatively inexpensive concoction called "staff," composed of jute, plaster of Paris, cement, glycerin, and dextrin. Although this composition was short-lived, when painted white it closely resembled a beautiful marble—hence the naming of the fair's "White City." Architects found this medium so adaptable that ultimately they used it to construct the complex's balustrades, basins, ornamental work, and even statuary. When the Exposition closed, these temporary constructions also proved easy to demolish, leaving no structural remnants of the fair in Jackson Park.

Each of the central theme buildings contained representative inventions and state-of-the-art examples from around the world; each literally became a temple of knowledge. Individual buildings for many states of the Union surrounded these central structures. The whole area was lit with 7,000 arc lights and 120,000 incandescent lamps—a tangible demonstration of the wonders of electricity. The "White City" stood as an antiseptic, futuristic promise to urbanites who daily fought pure-water and sanitation dangers.

Separate from, but complementing, the White City, organizers platted the Midway Plaisance. Formerly a roadway connecting Jackson Park with Washington Park, the Midway ran almost one mile by 600 feet wide. It mixed the ethnological exhibits of the Smithsonian Institution with model villages from such diverse places as Java and Germany and Japan.

Into this stew organizers turned all of the entertainment exhibits—from wild-animal performances to joy rides to "Little Egypt," the darling *coochee-coochee* dancer of the Nile. What they created was an amazing array of popular culture. The Midway Plaisance's mixture of entertainment and anthropology set the standard for world's fairs in the Twentieth Century. By offering exhibits of primitive cultures, the Midway also reinforced the Exposition's theme of American progress. In the United States, the future was destined to be brighter, better, and more harmonious.

Although the fabulous Columbian Exposition ran for only six months after its opening on the first of May 1893, the fair left a lasting imprint on the American cultural landscape. First, the event documented the fact that the Nineteenth Century was the greatest era of civilized progress in the history of the world. Second, it offered tangible examples of what technological progress would bring to American society—from the 260-foot-high Ferris wheel to a cylinder phonograph to carbonated soft drinks.

Finally, the fair promised a brighter future, for it tied national progress to the country's material growth and economic expansion. Implied in this presentation was the belief that continued American growth would produce an eventual utopia. In short, "bigger *would bring* better." This message proved especially attractive as the nation sunk deeper into economic depression. It also is the heart of the dichotomy presented by the author in *The Education of Henry Adams*. Adams developed the images of the Virgin and the dynamo after two trips to the fair in 1893.

In the face of an unstable economy, the Chicago Exposition became a rallying point for Americans. If so quickly Chicago could rebuild from a massive fire in 1871 and become the key metropolis of the Midwest, the possibility existed for any community, of any size, to succeed. The inspirational symbol of Chicago-as-phoenix was lost on no American. Chicago signified opportunity for America, and the Exposition provided the blueprint for that future.

Those Americans visiting the Chicago Exposition were the prime targets, but the entire population partook of the fair experience through newspaper and magazine accounts. Thus the organizers, from a two-square-mile site on Lake Michigan, imposed order on a national experience that held lasting implications for millions of Americans. Whether one attended the Exposition or not, he became a part of the national experience which the fair celebrated—and that experience was one of progress and technology and hope.

By the early 1890s, one of the most pervasive communication forms was syndicated copy in daily—and particularly weekly—newspapers. These columns of stereotype, preset on tin sheets, were called "ready-print" or "patent insides"—or, more derisively, "boilerplate." Depending upon the service to which the weekly editor subscribed, his prepared copy carried serialized stories, state news, humor, national news, agricultural information, or special-feature articles.

Although urban dailies had included this type of material for years, few weekly newspapers could afford it until the proliferation of stereotype companies in the 1880s. Even then, critics charged that such a publisher "edited his newspaper with a saw." Nevertheless, with the availability of stereotype plates, the weekly publisher offered a much wider choice of material to his readers, at a lower cost than if he had set the type himself. He gained not only flexibility of layout, but also greater control over his content. Very quickly the alert publisher realized that he needed ready-print material to remain competitive.

By the early 1890s, some of the larger stereotype-plate syndicates included the A. N. Kellogg Newspaper Company, the Western Newspaper Union, and the American Press Association. These national companies operated major newscopy offices in cities across the country and stringer offices in smaller cities. In 1893 they fought fiercely to sign the nation's 15,000 daily and weekly publishers.

Orlando Jay Smith had founded the American Press Association in 1882, when he was still the publisher of the *Chicago Express*. Soon he was supplying all kinds of features in plate form, by the page or by the column, to rural newspapers. His service proved so successful that he relocated in New York City and opened satellite offices in every major U.S. city, from Boston to Omaha to San Francisco. At the height of its business, the A.P.A. sold copy to more than two thirds of the publishers in the country.

Smith's approach to feature material involved assembling a stable of writers who either wrote regular columns for syndication or authored commissioned pieces on specific topics. Smith has been credited with starting on their careers, or furthering the popularity of, such notable writers as C. B. Lewis ("M. Quad"), Bill Nye, Eugene Field, Jack London, Booth Tarkington, and Thomas De Witt Talmage. Writing for the A.P.A., as for the other syndicates, proved lucrative by Victorian standards, and Smith guaranteed national exposure to an author.

Once Congress had chosen Chicago over New York, Washington, and St. Louis as the site of the World's Columbian Exposition, the editorial staff in Smith's A.P.A. office spawned a plan. They recalled the popular interest produced by the Centennial Exposition in Philadelphia (1876) and proposed a feature series that would benefit from a similar widespread interest in the Chicago extravaganza. As finally implemented, this plan provided 74 experts a platform from which to discuss aspects of American society a century hence. As conceived, each writer would be contributing to a "Chapter of Forecasts" focusing on the 1990s.

Some of these practiced observers would be members of the A.P.A.'s regular writing staff—for example, the humorist Bill Nye, the theologian Thomas De Witt Talmage, and the arts critic Octavus Cohen. The commentaries of other contributors the A.P.A. would commission individually—as those of politician William Jennings Bryan, capitalist George Westinghouse, Chicago mayor Hempstead Washburne, and political analyst Mary E. Lease.

As a result, the syndicate created a broad-spectrum commentary on life in the 1890s and a lexicon of predictions by noted Americans on life in the 1990s. The A.P.A. asked some of the more than six-dozen authors to confine themselves to specific topics. For example, Commissioner of Indian Affairs Thomas J. Morgan wrote solely on the future of the Native American, Methodist Bishop John Philip Newman confined his comments to Methodism in the 1990s, and entrepreneur Samuel Barton discussed only the commercial development of Florida.

The A.P.A. provided many of the other authors with a list of questions from which to select their topics. The result is a collection of topics as diverse as the "servant problem," the most revered American personality, and the future of fashionable dress. The list of proffered questions included:

1. What will be the state of medicine in the 1990s?

2. What will be the state of religion/theology in the 1990s?

3. What will be the state of great corporations and vast business aggregations in the 1990s?

4. What will be the condition and relationship of capital and labor in the 1990s?

5. Is the condition of the laboring class likely to become more or less dependent by the 1990s?

6. Will the tendency toward the accumulation of wealth in the hands of a few increase or diminish by the 1990s?

7. What will be the methods used to treat criminals in the 1990s?

8. What will be the state of common educational methods in the 1990s?

9. What will be the state of the newspaper press in the 1990s?

10. What will be the future of the servant problem?

11. What will be the future of fashionable dress in the Twentieth Century?

12. What is the future in temperance legislation in the United States?

13. What will be the state of the postal service in the 1990s?

14. What will be the state of transportation in the 1990s?

15. Is it likely that the railroads and telegraphs will be owned or managed by the state by the 1990s?

16. What changes in the structure and operation of the federal government will occur by the 1990s?

17. What will be the relation of political parties to the federal government, and to each other, in the Twentieth Century?

18. What will be the state of American music in the 1990s?

19. What will be the state of American drama in the 1990s?

20. What will be the state of American literature in the 1990s?

21. What changes do you foresee in the development of the South and the West?

22. Will there be any changes in the state of the American monetary system by the 1990s?

23. What developments do you foresee in the legal profession by the 1990s?

24. What will be the state of United States divorce laws in the 1990s?

25. Will our soil and methods of agriculture improve so as to provide food without difficulty for all of our population in the 1990s?

26. What will be the status of women—particularly regarding suffrage—in the 1990s?

27. What developments will most affect the American Indian in the Twentieth Century?

28. What will be the state of the English language in the 1990s?

29. What developments will occur in architecture by the 1990s?

30. What improvements, inventions, and discoveries in mechanics and industrial arts do you foresee by the 1990s?

31. Where will be the greatest city in America in the 1990s?

32. What American (now living) will be the most honored in the 1990s?

33. Will the race be happier, healthier, and handsomer in the 1990s than it is now?

Because this selection of questions is so wide-ranging, the A.P.A.'s stereotype-plate series on "America in the 1990s" is intriguing to readers at the end of the Twentieth Century. The syndicate packaged these essays in 11 weekly segments—each containing from 4 to 8 individual pieces. The segments ran in hundreds of the country's weeklies and in the Sunday feature section of scores of big-city dailies. The series began during the first week of March 1893, and concluded during the second week of May.

Thus the A.P.A. series drew hundreds of thousands of readers right into the World's Columbian Exposition. For the fair had opened on May 1, when President Grover Cleveland pressed a button in Washington, D.C., and machinery on the Exposition grounds roared into motion. Readers who had devoured the entire series were well-prepared for the startling features of the fair. In effect they had enrolled in a survey course on American social history—past, present, and future.

Each of the A.P.A.'s several dozen contributors to its "Chapter of Forecasts" approached his subject differently. Some writers discussed contemporary problems and prayed that they would be solved by the 1990s. Other authors isolated specific aspects of their 1890s society and projected these aspects into the future. Still other of the participants provided the ready-print syndicate with little more than their hopes for the future.

From the perspective of the 1990s, however, each of the 74 commentaries is a time-capsule nugget of insight. The insight may be into the author, rather than into his subject, but these writings are particularly revealing of both the author's background and his general perspectives. Each of these writers assumes the mantle of the seer, to a greater or lesser degree. In effect he becomes a predictor, a futurist.

The umbrella term "futurist" currently labels an array of predictors that runs from television/tabloid "personalities" who have predicted 13 of the last three political assassinations, to sensitive students of current developments who make projections compatible with the laws of nature. The ancestors of today's futurists—for example, George Orwell, R. Buckminster Fuller, Herman Kahn, and Isaac Asimov—faced the same difficulties in making realistic predictions.

Forecasters encounter difficulties when they extrapolate beyond the bounds of their current information. Sometimes these predictions can be couched in science fiction, as in the works of H. G. Wells. But there also is a compromise state that some futurists use to extend their convictions: the scenario. This mechanism combines fact with fiction and mixes hard forecasting with fantasy. Several of the A.P.A. writers relied on the scenario to extend their beliefs beyond their factual bases.

Between 1885 and 1900, almost 100 utopian novels were published. The majority of these works—like Edward Bellamy's *Looking Backward* and Ignatius Donnelly's *Caesar's Column*—use futuristic settings to comment on social deficiencies and reform. To some extent, these authors suffer from extending their legitimate forecasts into the realm of hopes and wishes. Both in the 1890s and today, much futuristic description rests on the heavily moral "how things *should* be," rather than on clear assessments of possible and potential technology.

Technology is the ultimate culprit in skewing most predictions. For few forecasters can divine the key invention (for example the automobile, or the atomic bomb, or the transistor) that will revolutionize American life 50 or 100 years hence. The futurist who can see such a key piece of technology, and can place it in a social context, becomes the true seer.

As with futurists closing the Twentieth Century, the 1890s A.P.A. writers frequently fell victim to two beliefs: that technology could and would solve society's problems; that human nature would change dramatically for the better. It is precisely these two beliefs that render some of the 1890s predictions the most outlandish. For technology is restricted by the laws of nature, as well as by socio-economic demands, and human nature is prone to change very little, if at all.

Today Then gives the reader an opportunity to glimpse into the past at his predecessors, as *they* attempted to peer into the future, at American life in the 1990s. To the reader is left the problem of assessing the validity of the predictions made by the American Press Association's 74 part-time futurists in 1892. This process is not simple, for it requires the reader to determine the current state of American society and life before making a judgment. Thus these selections reveal as much about American life in the 1990s as they do about American life in the 1890s.

To conclude his contribution in 1892, editor/author John Habberton remarked, "Perhaps I am wrong in some of these prophecies. But if that is so, I shall not be here to be twitted with it—now will I?"

Wrong, sir!

We have come to twit John Habberton!

Thomas De Witt
Talmage

**World Improving
All The Time**

At the time of writing this commentary, the Reverend Thomas De Witt Talmage (1832-1902) served the Central Presbyterian Church of Brooklyn, New York. He preached there weekly to large audiences drawn by his magnetic and rather sensational style. Talmage presented a strong, erect, clean-cut figure and used startling gestures and illustrations to rivet the attention of his listeners.

Born and schooled in New Jersey, Talmage blended the ministry with newspaper evangelism. At the height of his fame, in the 1890s, the pastor's sermons were published weekly in about 3,500 newspapers. Simultaneously he edited the Christian at Work *(1874-1876),* Frank Leslie's Sunday Magazine *(1881-1889), and the* Christian Herald *(1899-1902). He also authored numerous books, many of which used the sermon format. Talmage spent the last several years of his career at the First Presbyterian Church in Washington, D.C.—from which pulpit he commented on all aspects of American life.*

When you thrust me with more than 20 sharp interrogation points about what will be the condition of the world 100 years from now, I must first say that there is a possibility that the world by that time may be a heap of ashes or knocked to flinders.

All geologists agree in saying that the world is already on fire inside. All that Chicago saw of her big fire some 20 years ago was not a spark compared with the conflagration now raging in the hulk of this old ship of a world. And then the earthquakes—witness Charleston, and San Francisco, and Java. And then the comets shooting recklessly about, and the big chunks from other worlds falling in Kansas and Iowa, or picked up by the British Museum on the other side of the sea.

The fact is that our world needs to take out a policy with some astronomical fire-insurance or accident-insurance company. From the way the world goes on, it is certain something is the matter with it. The volcanoes are merely the regurgitation caused by internal cramps.

I am not apprehensive about the world, and I sleep well nights, and I do not want to frighten nervous people. However, considering what is going on down in the depths of the earth and what is flying all about us, I am surprised that the world has not long ago gone out of business. But suppose it lasts—and I hope it will, for it is a grand old world and worth saving—what, then, will be its condition in 1993?

In medicine? Well, cancer and consumption will be as easily cured as influenza or a "run round" [diarrhea].

Theology? Far more religion than now; the technicalities nothing; the spirit of religion dominant. The minister's war hatchet will be buried beside Modoc's tomahawk.

Condition of capital and labor? At peace, by the prevalence of the Golden Rule, which enjoins us to do to others as we would have them do to us.

Treatment of criminals? Prisons will have ventilation, and sunlight, and bathrooms, and libraries, and Christian influences that will be reformatory instead of damnatory.

Education methods? The stuffing machine that we call the school system, which is making the rising generation a race of invalids, will be substituted by something more reasonable. No more school girls with spectacles at 14, their eyes having been extinguished by overstudy, with overwrought brain. And no more boys in their dying dream trying to recite something in higher mathematics.

What American now living will be the most honored in 1993? By that time longevity will be so improved that 150 years will be no unusual age to reach. So I answer this question by saying that that American now sleeps in the cradle on the banks of the Hudson, or the Alabama, or the Oregon, or the Ohio—a rattle in hand, gum-swollen with a new tooth, and he will soon undertake a course of measles and mumps.

But he will pull through and advance, until I see him in 1993 presiding at a banquet. And, as he rises to speak, I hear him say, "Gentlemen, I was born in the latter part of the Nineteenth Century, and here we are in the latter part of the Twentieth, and the world has been improving all the time. And now I offer the toast for the evening. Charge your glasses with apollinaris water and drink deep to this sentiment:

"The newspaper press. May its influence in the Twenty-first Century be as happy and prosperous as in the Nineteenth and the Twentieth Centuries!"

James William
Sullivan

The Future Is A
Fancyland Palace

*By the early 1890s, Jim Sullivan (1848-1938) had parlayed his skill as a printer
into newspaper jobs across the country—including the editorship of the* Cheyenne
(Wyoming) Leader—*and had settled down in New York City. He became an active
follower of reformer Henry George and served (1887-1889) as the labor editor of George's
weekly* Standard. *Sullivan then led a successful national movement of legislative reform, translating the Swiss mechanisms of initiative and referendum to the progressive
American scene.*

*Much of Jim Sullivan's later career involved the labor movement, as he developed
a lasting friendship with Samuel Gompers, president of the American Federation of
Labor. He represented Gompers and the A.F.L. to European labor organizations, as
well as serving on national advisory commissions (1909-1924). Sullivan always showed
a natural scholarly bent, read widely, and wrote effectively on social and economic matters.
Most notably, he opposed any reform that might enlarge the role of the federal government.*

I find that I am unable to prophesy. The future is a fancyland palace whose
portals I cannot enter. Moving toward it from the Here, I am charmed with its
brilliant facade. What sculptured splendors—porticoes, pillars, statues, windows!
What is within?

As I advance, however, the airy structure recedes. I cannot push beyond its
threshold; its doors never open; on their other side are silence and mystery. I know
not what is there.

Today I was reading the prophesies of [Francois Noel] Babeuf. He was a French
revolutionary, a co-worker of [Maximilien Francois Marie Isidore de] Robespierre
and [the Marquis de] Condorcet. In 1792—possessed of fundamental sociologic
truths, and inspired by the political progress of the times—he foretold for 1892

27

the abolition of rank, of poverty, of social injustice. He saw clearly the relation of land to labor and the manifold benefits of cooperation. He expected all the world soon to see what he did. So he described a dreamer's 1892—but we beheld the 1892 of fact.

Yet, let us listen to today's visionaries and dreamers. For they are pleasing fellows:

There is imaginative [former U.S. Postmaster General] John Wanamaker. He foresees a one-cent letter for all the postal union; a free-mail delivery in every country district; a short-hour day for post-office employees; a cheap national telegraph and telephone service.

The poet of a pure democracy [Charles A.] Dana predicts legislation by all the citizens in every political body corporate. He fancies that all the electors in the United States may vote directly—"yea" or "nay"—on the tariff, on silver coinage, on a national banking system, on the restriction of immigration. From New England and Swiss experiences, he infers that real democracy is the best policy, even for the whole Union.

Another bold theorist is [Central Pacific Railroad executive] C. P. Huntington. He assures us of wondrous millions to be saved in railroad consolidation. What, then, if all our trunk railroads were under a single management?

President [Archibald A.] McLeod, of Reading, is out with a financial suggestion. The consumer of coal, he says, will be benefited if the great coal operator (Mr. McLeod's railroad) performs the complete work of producing coal—from digging it to delivering it in the consumer's cellar. The plan abolishes retail agents, reduces the working force otherwise, and permits just one general superintendency.

Those audacious revolutionists [Philip Danforth] Armour and [John D.] Rockefeller have actually evinced glimmerings of practicability! From central headquarters they control vast organized systems of meat and oil distribution. Shall our people ever again go back to petty local methods? Never! These businesses are now adjusted to a national scale.

Many enthusiasts are at work in lesser circles of social reform. [Frederick William] DeVoe, for 20 years the superintendent of New York's markets, wrote a book to show that a public market in each ward would reduce the price of country produce to the householder by 20 percent or so. The department-store proprietors are forever entertaining wilder schemes to be applied in cheapening shop goods. The unconservative street-railroad system, with its cables and trolleys, has brought the average cost of the passenger's ride (to the syndicate) down to 2 cents.

Ah, if the great public would take to dreaming with these dreamers, planning for itself as they do for themselves, and taking up with their ways of doing business, how rich and happy it might be in 1993!

W. R. Grace

A Great Era For South America

One of the consummate capitalists of his day, William Russell Grace (1832-1904) succeeded as an international merchant and a concessionaire. Grace became a pioneer of economic imperialism in an era when the United States was just feeling its way into international commerce. The young Irishman grew up with ties to South America, specifically through his father's support of Venezuelan independence. William moved from Peru to New York City (1865), where he organized W. R. Grace and Company, a general-merchandising firm with international ties. Grace and his brother became the prime suppliers to the Peruvian government during the late 1870s.

Known as "the Pirate of Peru" to his critics, W. R. Grace managed Peruvian concessions into a massive mercantile organization. In 1895 the various Grace companies united under a Virginia charter. The firm then developed worldwide contacts, with extensive import, export, and banking operations in South America. Grace also assumed the role of philanthropist, however, and he maintained an interest in American politics. Interestingly, in 1880, W. R. Grace had been elected the first Roman Catholic mayor of New York City.

I look for very great changes, all of them in the direction of business prosperity in American commercial development, in the next century. I expect to see a great merchant marine, although I am one of those who believe that this cannot be procured by us until there are changes in our navigation laws. The substitution of iron and steel for wood, and of steam for sail power—which has been going on with great rapidity in the past 20 years—accounts partly, I think, for the decadence in American shipping.

And if Congress shall so legislate that Americans can compete with foreign shipowners, there is likely to be a revival of American shipping interest and ship-building, as well as the development of a race of American sailors like those of former times. They were as fine sailors as trod the decks, and simultaneously they were distinguished from all other seamen by their business ability.

The development of the great West, and especially of the South and the Southwest will, I think, be as prodigious in the early part of the coming century as has been that of the states of the Ohio Valley under the influence of railway construction. I am inclined to think that the American farmer must either find new wheat lands by a well-considered and elaborate general system of irrigation or special methods of cultivation. Or else the American people will be compelled in the next century to import instead of export wheat.

On the other hand, the active men of the Twentieth Century are going to see a magnificent development of corn and other cereals in the fertile lands of the great Southwest. And American genius is going to show Europe how nu-tritive and desirable American corn is for food purposes when it is properly cooked. For that reason we shall probably find that our exports of corn will more than make up for the falling off in the exports of wheat.

But I think that one of the greatest commercial developments is going to be, so far as the United States is concerned, in the relations between this country and those of the South American continent. The Andes Mountains are already surmounted by a railroad which is going to open up that magnificent plateau,

GOVERNMENT BUILDING.

or montane, which stretches to the eastward from the Andes.

As fine a cotton country as there is in the world is there and, with the opening of this railroad, a particularly fine grade of cotton will be developed. There are millions of acres suitable for tobacco culture, and higher up there is a wheat belt of virgin soil almost as large as is the great wheat belt of the United States.

Besides, there are the great silver mines of the Cerro de Pasco. These were known even from the time of the Incas, which history has so many romances about. By the record of taxation, these mines have produced over $420,000,000 since the conquest.

Now men are living who will see this enormous land brought under development. This change will bring the South American countries into closer relation with the United States. There will be competition, of course, but some competition of this sort ought not be unhealthy.

And I presume that, in the next century, there may be built a railway reaching so far that it may be possible to enter a palace car in New York City and ride it to Lima, Santiago, Rio de Janeiro, or Buenos Aires. Railroad development will do for South America what it has done for the United States.

And the activity of our commerce will bring the United States into very close alliance with the southern continent and will cause a development of commercial relations the consequences of which cannot be realized today. The Twentieth Century is going to be a great era for South America, and that continent cannot flourish without benefiting the United States.

I am one of those who believe that the commercial and manufacturing development of this country during the Twentieth Century will be such that the genius of the American people will make it perfectly possible for this country to compete successfully with all the great manufacturing centers of Europe. This will be done with a great majority of the classes of goods that are now being marketed by England, France, and Germany—not only in South America, but in all the great centers of commerce throughout the world.

T. V.
Powderly

No Very Rich
Or Very Poor

From a Pennsylvania background, Terence Vincent Powderly (1849-1924) left school at an early age to work on the railroad. Once apprenticed as a mechanic, he immersed himself in statewide labor organizing. Powderly aligned himself with the Knights of Labor and rose to a leadership role in this group by the early 1890s. As the mayor of Scranton, Pennsylvania (1878-1884), he also understood the difficulties of management.

In an age of Populism, Powderly became an outspoken advocate of the government ownership of public utilities, the regulation of trusts and monopolies, and reform of the currency and the land systems. His ultimate goal remained the abolition of the wage system. A fluent and nimble-witted orator, Powderly wove these reforms into many of his public addresses and his several labor publications.

Always an active student, the labor leader studied law and was admitted to the Pennsylvania bar in 1894. In the 1890s, Powderly campaigned heroically for the Republican ticket and, in return, received a series of positions in the U.S. Bureau of Immigration. A relentless reformer, Powderly frequently mixed his heart-felt desires with his assessments of reality.

Three millions celebrated in 1793, 63,000,000 in 1893, and 300,000,000 will in 1993 celebrate the landing of Columbus. They will be educated and refined, for the arts and sciences will be taught in the public schools. Not only will the mind of the pupil be trained, but the hand as well. Each child will be instructed in the manual of tools.

They will be instructed in the functions of every part of the human system; "man, know thyself" will have a meaning in 1993. The economic and social questions of the day will also be taught in the schools. There will be no uneducated persons to act as drags on the car of progress.

The form of government will be simpler, and the initiative and referendum will prevail. Lawmakers will not be the autocrats they now are, for they will truly register the will of the people. They will not dictate to them, as at present.

The commonwealth will be organized on industrial lines. Labor organizations will have disappeared, for there will be no longer a necessity for their existence. An ideal democracy will stand upon the foundations that we of 1893 are erecting.

Railroads, water courses, telegraphs, telephones, pneumatic tubes, and all

other methods of transporting passengers, freight, and intelligence will be owned and operated by the government. The earnings of these agencies will swell the public treasury. Homes will flourish, for they will no longer be taxed. Instead of devoting so much time and money to the erecting of great public structures, as at present, the erection and adornment of the home will receive first consideration.

Each home will be regarded as a contribution to the wealth and beauty of the nation. The earnings of public concerns will defray the cost of maintaining streets, sewers, waterworks, and light- and heat-giving establishments. Cremation will take the place of the present system of burying the dead. And the living will be healthier, for the earth will not be poisoned through the interment of infection. The contents of sewers will not flow into river and stream to send deadly vapors through the air, but will be utilized to enrich the harvest-yielding earth.

The progress of the lower grades of animal life has been skillfully guided and hastened, until we may now assert that cattle and fowl are approaching perfection. In 1993 the same attention will be bestowed on the human race. Instead of rushing blindly forward, increasing and multiplying at haphazard, humanity will knowingly and intelligently advance to higher altitudes.

There will be no very rich or very poor, for—long before 1993 dawns upon the world—the industrialists will have learned that the raising of large families is but another way to create slaves to perform the drudgery of the wealthy. And the family will be restricted to the capacity of the parents to maintain and educate it.

Under such conditions, prisons and poorhouses will decline, and divorces will not be considered necessary. The system which makes criminals of men and women—and at the same time makes millionaires of the others—will have disappeared. As a consequence, the confinement and punishment of criminals will occupy but little of the thought or time of the men of 1993.

A. M.
Palmer

Distinctly American Drama Will Come

At a time when the best American drama merely imitated the European stage, Albert Marshman Palmer (1838-1905) proved a quiet innovator. Palmer graduated from the New York University Law School in 1860, but he never practiced. Rather, he joined the post-Civil War theater scene in New York City as a production manager. During a 30-year career, Palmer built a reputation as a first-rate theatrical executive, whose productions contained both vigor and vitality.

Albert Palmer first managed the Union Square Theatre in New York City (1872-1883). He then owned and operated the Madison Square Theatre (1883-1891) and Wallack's Theatre (1891-1896), which he renamed Palmer's. Contemporaries recognized Palmer as a prime patron of native drama—supporting American playwrights, American actors, and American touring companies. His most permanent contribution to the field, however, was the founding of the Actor's Fund of America, of which he served as president for 14 years.

I presume that the Americans will create a drama as artistic, as perfect, and of as great an influence as that which has characterized the national drama of France. The indications all point that way.

Hitherto we have had almost no distinctively American drama. We have had only artists—some of whom are quite as impressive and talented as some of those who have made the fame of the French stage. I do not need to mention them, every one knows who they are.

We have learned already how to mount a play, how to give it all those accessories which combine to furnish the perfect representation. And yet, after all, we have been compelled to depend, if not entirely upon the greater dramatists of Europe, at least upon the methods and the suggestions indicated by the work of those who are esteemed the greater dramatists.

Until recently I may say that we have had no distinctively American play. Some of the American dramatists have written plays which have been great successes and are models of dramatic workmanship. And yet, after all, these plays have 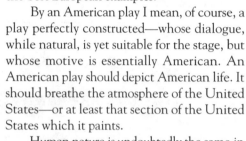 been written and constructed in imitation of the best European examples.

By an American play I mean, of course, a play perfectly constructed—whose dialogue, while natural, is yet suitable for the stage, but whose motive is essentially American. An American play should depict American life. It should breathe the atmosphere of the United States—or at least that section of the United States which it paints.

Human nature is undoubtedly the same in all countries and in all ages, but the manifestations or developments of it have the flavor of locality. It is the art of the playwright, while setting forth human nature, to set it forth so that both its truth is recognized and its environment is suggested faithfully. That is what the coming American playwright must do and, I believe, will do.

American life furnishes every material for the perfect drama, the exquisite pure comedy, or the more amusing and yet not necessarily less faithful low comedy. Recently we have had one or two plays of this kind. The tendency of today unquestionably is for amusement, and that broad amusement which evokes hearty laughter.

It is quite likely that, in the next century, the demand may be for higher ideals than this. And when this demand comes, I have no doubt that the American playwright will be found who will meet it. In the Twentieth Century, the American drama ought to rank with those of the golden days of the drama of the Old World.

Ella Wheeler
Wilcox

Splendid Amazons And Pygmy Men

Throughout her long career as a poet, Ella Wheeler Wilcox (1850-1919) enjoyed great popularity. Ella Wheeler was born in Johnstown Center (near Madison), Wisconsin, and showed a remarkable aptitude for writing at a young age. With her family's encouragement, Ella began to publish her poems in national magazines before she was 16 years old; by 20, she brought a tidy supplement to the family income.

In 1884 Ella married Robert Marius Wilcox, a producer of art in silver, and the couple moved to Connecticut. Although they travelled widely, Ella continued to write both prose and poetry for national publication. She ultimately published more than 30 volumes and, at one point in the early 1890s, she produced a daily poem for national newspaper syndication.

Although some critics found Wilcox's work platitudinous and sentimental, she argued that it brought comfort and hope to millions of Americans in dire circumstances. Her message remained one of unwavering optimism, mixed with theosophy and the occult.

In 1993 the government will have grown more simple, as true greatness tends always toward simplicity. Railroads and telegraphs will belong to the state, thus lessening the dangerous power of large monopolies and vast corporations. Otherwise, in less than a century, our boasted American freedom would cease to exist, since it is already menaced.

In temperance the world ere then will have realized the folly of trying to legislate upon appetites. It will realize the necessity of educating drunkards—and that to educate them we must begin with parents. People who refuse to be taught on this and kindred subjects must be prevented from becoming parents. In this way only can drunkenness be lessened.

The same humane law will, by that time, extend to criminals—they will be prevented from propagating their kind. This will take the place of capital punishment and, after a few generations, will do away with crime, because no criminals will be born.

The whole vast West will be irrigated and fertilized, furnishing food for all our population. Architecture will have reached a much higher state, but it will not in 500 years attain the perfection found in countries thousands of years old. Airships will facilitate travel, and the pneumatic tube will be the means of transporting goods.

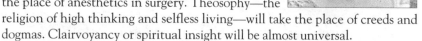

America will produce the greatest authors who shall be living in 1993. In musical achievement it will still be behind older countries.

The occult sixth sense will be the predominant element in medicine and theology. Mesmerism will take the place of anesthetics in surgery. Theosophy—the religion of high thinking and selfless living—will take the place of creeds and dogmas. Clairvoyancy or spiritual insight will be almost universal.

Woman will be financially independent of man, and this will materially lessen crime. No longer obliged to rifle her husband's pockets for money, she will not give birth to kleptomaniacs or thieves. Men will learn the importance of proper prenatal conditions, and children will be reared with the same care now given to colts, calves, and dogs.

The government will establish colleges for the training of servants. And architects will consider the comfort and health of domestics in constructing homes, instead of ignoring them, as at present. Better instructed, better paid, better cared for, and more plentiful, the servant of the next century will be more useful, better content, and more respectful and respected.

If our men keep pace with our women in athletic development and in clean morals, the race will be larger and handsomer. Otherwise we shall produce splendid amazons and pygmy men.

Chicago will be our greatest city because she knows she is not, and desires to be, and has the energy and zeal to become so. Each of our other large cities thinks she is already the greatest and will make no pronounced effort to be greater. All permanent greatness means eternal endeavor.

If any man now living solves the great question of the true relation of capital and labor, to him will 1993 accord the honor of the greatest man. Next to him stands [Thomas] Edison.

Bill
Nye

I Speak From Experience

By the early 1890s, Edgar Wilson "Bill" Nye (1850-1896) had become one of the most recognized personalities in America. Born in Maine and raised in Wisconsin, Nye read law and then went west, to be admitted to the Wyoming bar in 1876. Although he never practiced law, the degree gained Nye the positions of justice of the peace and later postmaster of Laramie. At the same time Nye wrote for a series of western newspapers, including his own Laramie Boomerang *(1881-1884). For health reasons, Nye moved east in 1886 and took a position as columnist for the* New York World, *with which he was associated the remainder of his life. Beginning in 1885, Nye also launched a career as a public lecturer. With a series of more serious foils, the humorist toured the nation to packed houses and rave reviews.*

A newspaper syndicate dispersed Nye's columns from coast to coast, and his self-deprecating humor earned him distinction in the literary school of Mark Twain and Artemus Ward. Nye brought to American humor a Western perspective of broad kindness and open humanity—characteristics still available to readers of his books.

Politically there will be far less money expended in electing officials, I fancy. And many of our leading politicians out of a job will be living on the island [incarcerated], while those now on the island will have learned that the price of one vote will not maintain them for four years. All these things will elevate society and throw what is now called "society" out of a job.

The government will grow simpler. So will the men who now overestimate their wisdom.

The government should own both railways and telegraphs, no doubt. But how the transfer could be made so as to avoid a large steal, while the state is looking out of the window, I do not know. It would be a good time now to buy some railroads I know of—roads that are never on time but once a year, and that is when they put on extra steam in order to pass a dividend.

I believe that in our monetary system the same change will be maintained, though more of it perhaps.

I think less attention will be paid to temperance legislation and more to the study of the human stomach. Bad cooking, especially as we find it in poor hotels on the road, is the parent of many drunkards. You cannot legislate nice, new, iron-gray brains or good stomachs into people who have acquired (by descent or purchase) weak, inflamed, and diseased ones. If you could, the legislature would have very little time to work outside of the Capitol building.

I do not see any practical way of punishing prisoners at present, but I am liable to think of one at any time.

The laws of divorce are quite well adapted to this age. The only improvement I see would be for people who apply for divorce to pay regular advertising rates instead of displaying free to the public their private bone works in order to boom a new play or a new star.

I see no reason to hope that money will not accumulate in the hands of a few in the future, even more than in the past. There also will be more generations between shirt sleeves and shirt sleeves.

Vast corporations and business aggregations may become top heavy and cumbersome. With threatened strikes or actual trouble of that kind, capital may fight shy of them inside of 100 years.

The laboring classes will always be oppressed.

And the more their wages are increased, the more fatigued they will feel. I speak from experience.

Our soil, with improved agricultural methods, should grow enough for an increased population. But I hope that the government will not depend too much on me. I farmed last year in North Carolina and bought hay for my horses and canned food for my family. And I used condensed milk on those days when my valet milked our spirited cow by scaring her half way over a barbed-wire fence and then attending to her dividend arrangement, while the bawling or intellectual end hung over the other side.

Law, medicine, and theology will continue to advance as rapidly as they have the past 100 years, especially theology. We will continue to talk saucily to all three until we meet them, and then we will retract all that we have said. I see more possibilities for medicine, however, than for the rest.

American literature, I hope, will be more realistic in 100 years. And it will be, I trust, as good in the daily press at two cents as in the more elaborate and expensive publications. I trust there will be less colic among poets, and less vain regret and gastritis among poetesses.

Music and the drama will grow rapidly. The great American play has been already written by Mr. [Bronson] Howard, and a new era is about to be opened. I may open one myself.

Educational methods will go on toward perfection. Finally the pupil will not have to apply himself at all—but the teacher's work will grow more and more laborious.

Dress, I hope, will be simplified for the day-time. Evening dress, however, could not be made any more simple than it is without carrying the entire train and waistband in one hand and getting a check for it at the door. Man will dress as usual, paying eight dollars twice each year for a high hat that has just change enough in it to compel him to buy one every six months. He will also wear other clothing, but it will be simple and not so close-fitting.

The architecture will advance in great cities. And the architects will go on making pretty drawings of dwelling houses, which will not have any closets, and the hall will contain the wood-box and the lavatory, as it does now.

Women will never want the right of suffrage—that is, there will not be enough of them that want it to even encourage the menfolks to give it to them.

The future of the servant problem is the same as the future of the ungodly—viz., hell.

I look for the perfection of the flying machine, but fear it will arrive too late to be of practical use to lecturers.

"Will the race be handsomer, healthier, or happier than it is now?" I certainly hope so!

Our greatest city will be on the present site of Chicago.

As to who will be the American most honored in 1993, I am offering odds that it will not be the son of a wealthy man, but some poor boy at present with chapped wrists and chilblains on his heels, whose heart is full of hope and whose terror now is soap.

Of course the people will not have forgotten [George] Washington. And I am also putting up a delicate little tribute to myself in the way of a mausoleum, which will resist climatic action and keep me as green as ever in the memory of those from whom I am liable now to be snatched away at any moment.

William H. H.
Miller

More Harmonious Divorce Laws

In 1889 William Henry Harrison Miller (1840-1917) reached the peak of his legal career, when President Benjamin Harrison appointed him Attorney General of the United States. After service in the Union Army, Miller had read law in Indiana and was admitted to the bar in 1865. His early career proved so promising that Harrison offered Miller a partnership in his Indianapolis law firm. Miller earned a reputation as an honest, impartial, well-schooled attorney.

When Harrison won election (1888), his appointment of Miller was surprising, as his partner was virtually unknown outside Indiana. Yet Miller became a solid Attorney General, who enforced laws vigorously and impartially, without regard to political influences. Upon completing his term, Miller returned to Indianapolis, where he practiced until 1910.

The next 100 years will bring few changes in our federal government. He would be a rash man who should positively predict that conditions will not arise which might make a change of some radical nature imperative, but I can see no signs of such a necessity. In minor respects there will be changes and modifications, no doubt, such as are suggested by experience. In fact, some changes are already known to be desirable.

A century hence I should expect to see the divorce laws of the country, for instance, much more harmonious than they are at the present time. But I believe our divorce laws will continue to be the enactment of states and not of the federal Congress. I am as much of a believer as any one in what is called centralization of power for all national purposes. But I cannot believe that divorce, or the regulation of divorce, can be made to appear in any proper sense a national question. What is not truly national should be left to the states.

It is true that the lack of uniformity in the divorce laws of the states is at the present time a crying evil. It tempts to corruption and at best produces confusion in the courts and sometimes consternation in the marriage relations of individuals. The remedy for this will be found, I think, during the coming 100 years in the perfection of the divorce laws of the states, after what shall appear to be the best models. Instinctively and for the good of the people of their own state, legislators will adopt the statues of those commonwealths which have secured best results, or at best imitate them.

It is possible, though I am not willing to say probable, that Congress may promote the much-desired homogeneity of divorce laws by some act designed to give greater force to that section of the Constitution which provides that "full faith and credit shall be given in each state to the public acts, records, and judicial proceedings of every other state."

It is from lack of such credit in some state courts to the acts of other state courts that much of the confusion in divorce matter proceeds. The Constitution expressly authorizes Congress to apply a remedy in such cases, adding, "And the Congress may by general laws prescribe the manner in which such acts, records, and proceedings shall be proved, and the effect thereof." Under this authority Congress might and probably should enact some law that will make obligatory the giving in each state of full faith and credit in divorce proceedings and legislation in other states.

MANUFACTURES AND LIBERAL ARTS BUILDING.

Thomas J.
Morgan

The Indian Tribes
Will Disappear

In 1892, Thomas Jefferson Morgan (1839-1902) sat at the center of both social and political turmoil involving Native Americans. As President Benjamin Harrison's Commissioner of Indian Affairs (1889-1893), Morgan became the target of myriad factions, each with an agenda for the American Indian. Some of Morgan's frustrations are apparent in his predictions concerning "the Indian in 1993."

Schooled in Indiana, Morgan had served in the Union forces during the Civil War—most notably as a recruiter of African-American troops and as lieutenant colonel of the 14th U.S. Colored Infantry. After leaving the Army, Morgan graduated from the Rochester (New York) Theological Seminary (1868) and was ordained a Baptist minister. He found employment, however, in a series of educational administrative positions on the East Coast. Perhaps Morgan's greatest success as Commissioner of Indian Affairs involved his enforced separation of church and state in regard to Indian schools. After his government service, Morgan gained additional recognition as the secretary of the American Baptist Home Mission Society. He served in this capacity until his death.

I have been asked to set forth what changes are likely to take place in the status of the American Indians during the coming century. It must be confessed that I have considerably less confidence in my prophetic ability than I had before the last Presidential election [November 1892]. But, as no one of the 65,000,000 people of this country will ever know whether my prophecy proves true or false, I may venture to indulge my imagination with some degree of impunity.

The number of Indians at the present time is about 250,000. A hundred years hence, they will number a million or so. This increase will be due to the cessation of wars, the spread of intelligence and morality, the improvement of hygienic conditions, the disappearance of the medicine man, the better food supply, and the inter-marriage with whites. [The 1990 U.S. Census counted 1,959,000 Native Americans; individual tribes or nations set their own criteria for enrollment.]

Meanwhile some tribes will become wholly extinct, leaving scarcely a trace of their history outside of the records of the Indian Bureau. Other tribes, like the Sioux and Navajo, will rapidly increase and will retain most of their characteristic traits. The Pueblos of New Mexico (who currently are rejecting so successfully the efforts of the government in their behalf) will continue to be a favorite people for the ethnologists and the self-ostracized journalists who find pleasure and profit in barbarism.

There will be here and there wandering bands of blanket beggars. These aboriginal tramps will perpetuate the absurdities and enormities of Indian life either as a profession or as a providential object lesson for students of history. These students will thus be able to form a fair estimate of the great work that the Indian Bureau has wrought in helping to redeem the great mass of the Indians.

The tribes will disappear and the agencies will become a thing of the past, thus disposing of the much-abused Indian agents, whether civilians or Army officers. The friction between the Interior and the War Departments will be produced by other causes.

And Army officers, having no longer an excuse for trying to run the Indian Office, will seek other fields for the exercise of their talents. Further, the said Indian Office—that inexhaustible source of news when all sources fail—will be forever closed, the Indian Commissioner will have a rest, and the Catholics and penny-a-liners [newspaper correspondents] on mischief bent will have to hunt for other targets.

The great body of Indians will become merged in the indistinguishable mass of our population. And there will spring up a new aristocracy, claiming distinction by reason of Indian descent. To be able to trace one's pedigree back to some great warrior or big chief, or to have the right to claim descent from one of the first graduates of Carlisle, will be almost as desirable as to belong to New York's "Four Hundred."

Many Indians will achieve distinction as orators, poets, financiers, and inventors. Some of the finest poetry ever penned will find its inspiration and material in Indian history. And a whole generation of novelists will win fame and favor by stories whose leading characters are of Indian descent. Chicago University will proudly boast of an Indian laboratory devoted to Indian life and language.

An Indian will command the United States Army. Another will be our minister to Spain and have the honor of inviting the royal party to attend the centennial fair, to be held in Denver in 1992.

With the disappearance of the Indians will disappear the Indian Rights Association—or it will turn its ever-watchful eye to the condition of the perhaps-still "heathen Chinee." Thus the Army will gladly abandon the plains and take up its permanent abode in the ever-desired haven of Washington.

Miriam
Leslie

The Era Of Woman
As A Power
Has Commenced

Miriam Florence Folline Leslie (c. 1836-1914) spoke in the early 1890s with a firm base in iconoclasm. Born in Louisiana and raised in New York City, she married twice before working as an editor in Frank Leslie's magazine office. Miriam married the famed publisher in 1874, and the two travelled widely and lived lavishly.

Following her husband's bankruptcy (1877) and death (1880), Miriam Leslie assumed the management of the publishing business and erased its $300,000 deficit. In 1882 she legally changed her name to "Frank Leslie." Her ultimate resurrection of the Leslie company gained widespread admiration in the business world. She also wrote numerous volumes, including travelogues, social commentaries, and suffrage tracts. An ardent feminist, Miriam Leslie willed the bulk of her fortune to the cause of woman's suffrage.

To my mind the world, and more especially the New World, is hastening rapidly toward iconoclasm. Monarchs who used to be worshipped as gods and later on were so feared and misapprehended that the people slew them—to save themselves from some terrible extermination—are now only laughed at. Their natural disappearance from the scene now is foretold with as little awe as is felt in speaking of the destruction of the bison or the "noble savage."

Religion, another grand conservator of the distinction of classes, is unfortunately ceasing to be a power in the world. It has become, rather, the recreation of a small portion of the people.

Dress, formerly a species of trademark placed by the nations upon their population, is rapidly losing its individuality all over the world. The Turk has exchanged his turban for the silk hat, and the Tyrolean maiden wears a very far-off imitation of an old Parisian fashion.

Language is struggling toward universality. Almost anyone can now make himself understood almost anywhere.

In politics the people as a controlling power are coming to the front more or less rapidly in even the oldest empires of earth. And it needs no prophet to foretell that in 1993 the world will have become equalized in every respect, even to dire monotony.

The position of woman at the end of another century is a matter very easy to perceive and very difficult to formulate. That the era of woman as a power has commenced, even the shortest vision must discern. Her advancement has been as solid and as irresistible as that of the dames des halle upon the royalties of Versailles, and the spectator holds his breath, muttering, "And then?"

I speak impersonally—being one of those women whose hands have always been too full to allow her to grasp at any more rights than they held. But as I glance across the field of the Twentieth Century, I stand in awe of the possibilities of the reign of woman there displayed.

The "servant problem" is an imminent one, for no one is found to dispute that anarchy in domestic matters is the near result of the present attitude of the domestic official. I am inclined to prophesy that a species of "civil service" will be the result. Centralization is the law of the future, and a paternal government must establish domestic depots where every class of servants shall be trained and placed under stringent regulations.

In fact, both employers and employed will be subject to laws which both classes will be instrumental in framing. It is a possibility, but I do not undertake just here to formulate it, leaving that to the wise heads of 1950.

George
Westinghouse

Railroads: Uniform Speed Is The Answer

The career of George Westinghouse (1846-1914) keys the Industrial Age in America.
The inventor and manufacturer was born in New York and schooled locally, until serving
with the Union forces in the Civil War. Westinghouse then returned to his father's machine
shop, where—at the age of 19—he developed a rotary engine and received the first of
his more than 400 patents.

The young man's first major contribution was his invention of the air brake and
its application to railroading. The development of the Westinghouse Air Brake Company
led him to apply the standardization of equipment to American industry. Westinghouse
thereafter invented and developed basic systems for railroad signalling, natural-gas trans-
portation, and alternating-current power transmission.

In 1893 the Westinghouse Electric Company had contracted to light the World's
Columbian Exposition in Chicago and to develop the power of Niagara Falls. Despite
financial difficulties encountered in the Crash of 1907, George Westinghouse main-
tained his optimism, his courage, and his confidence. To his death, he never lost ei-
ther his imagination or his ability to solve a complex problem.

There is no question about the development of a much higher rate of speed
than that which even the fastest service on the railroads of today maintain. I
presume that a speed of from 90 to 100 miles an hour could be secured with modern
locomotives and with the improvements which are sure to come. [In 1992, Amtrak's
Metroliner, the fastest U.S. train, reaches a top speed of 125 miles an hour.]

But I am inclined to think that other influences in the next century may
operate to prevent the running of railway trains at such a speed as I have seen
mentioned in some of the newspapers. It is not a question of attaining speed,
but a question of the control of the train after great speed has been secured. Suppose,

for instance, that a railway train is going at the rate of 90 miles an hour. And then the engineer sees a danger signal or an obstruction on the track 1,000 feet away.

Now, experiments have shown that, with a perfect brake acting under the most perfect conditions, it is impossible to procure a greater retarding effect than would be equivalent to stopping a train going at the rate of 3 miles an hour in a second of time. It is, therefore, easy to make a computation of the effect of such a brake upon a train running 90 miles an hour within 1,000 feet.

When the engineer had reached the danger signal or the obstruction, his train would still be going at the rate of 60 miles an hour. And, even if he was running his engine at the rate of 60 miles, he could only check it to a rate of something like 40 miles an hour within that distance.

For this reason I am inclined to think that the development of railway travel in the next century along the present lines will be not so much great speed as uniform speed. The ideal speed, I think, will be about 40 miles an hour and steadily maintained from the time of leaving one terminal to the time of arrival at the destination. That will give most satisfactory results.

A steady speed of 40 miles an hour would enable a train to run from New York to Chicago in a little over 20 hours and with greater economy and far less danger. It is my impression, therefore, that railway travel in the next century will take on this development rather than high rates of speed.

I am also satisfied that the immense cost of furnishing power for electric railways—which some persons seem to think can secure and maintain a speed of 100 miles an hour and more—will make such a development commercially unprofitable. Although there is no doubt that electricity as a motive power for passenger traffic will be extensively used in the next century.

Asa C.
Matthews

The United States
of the Americas

*At the time Asa Carrington Matthews (1833-1908) prepared his forecast of the
United States in the 1990s, he was serving as the First Comptroller of the U.S. Treasury—
yet another position of public responsibility for this diverse attorney. Matthews was born
and schooled in Pike County, Illinois. He joined the bar in 1857 and then performed
heroically in the Civil War, particularly at Vicksburg. After the war he returned to his
practice in Pittsfield, specializing in reclamation and other agricultural law.*

*Colonel Matthews was elected to three terms in the Illinois Legislature, and he served
as Speaker of the House for one assembly. A staunch Republican, he was appointed
a regional Internal Revenue collector and a director of the Illinois Vicksburg Military
Park Commission, prior to his selection for the Washington, D.C., post. Throughout his varied career, Matthews demonstrated "a fidelity of purpose that commanded the respect of all." He proved an eminently solid fellow.*

I think that I can see, a hundred years hence, an ocean-bound republic over
every part of which the Stars and Stripes will proudly wave. Looking to the future,
my eye detects on the dim horizon an American republic which shall embrace
not only the present United States and Alaska, but all the remainder of the North
American continent now under British, Mexican, or minor domination. It seems
to me that this is the destiny of America—to come under one government, to
have but one flag, to be one people.

Such consolidation of power and unification of interest will of course make
the greatest empire that the sun ever shone upon. It will be an empire unrivaled
in ancient or modern times in population, in climatical favor, in physical resources,
and in the intelligence and patriotism of its people.

Isolated to some extent from the remainder of the world, we shall have little danger of entangling alliances or of troublesome contact. There will be no disputes about boundary lines, about seal or fish or bait. There will be no international railway question to harass our statesmen or to unsettle trade. This great ocean-bound American republic will maintain a navy superior to anything else afloat, simply as a matter of precaution.

There will be free trade throughout the North American continent and possibly free trade with all the world. As to when I cannot say, nor even hazard an opinion—though I am satisfied that, if free trade or freer trade shall come, it will not be for many years. And it cannot possibly come until every important industry existing or possible, throughout the length and breadth of the new and larger republic, has been planted firmly upon a basis of enduring prosperity.

Such a government will be strong enough to protect even the humblest of its citizens and to develop every resource. It will be a government of perhaps 60 states of the Union.

In the form of government, I do not expect to see much change from the present. The human mind has not yet devised improvements upon our present form which are likely to commend themselves to any considerable portion of the people. And yet it is a comfort to know that we have the elasticity which will enable us easily and peacefully to adapt ourselves to any new conditions that may arise. For 100 years or more to come, however, I expect to see our present form of government substantially preserved—and extended gradually over Mexico, Canada, and British America, as well as the states of Central America.

This will be an empire with the greatest railways (steam or electrical), canals and waterways, cities, farms, homes, colleges, factories, telegraphs, telephones, and all the new and wondrous things which a century of invention may bring us. For this will be the most perfect civilization and the most prosperous and happy people that the world ever knew.

John Clark
Ridpath

Aluminum: Shining
Symbol Of The Age

*One of the most popular writers of historical works of his time was John Clark Ridpath
(1840-1900). This prolific author, raised in Indiana, graduated from Indiana Asbury
University (1863) and taught in local schools until 1869. At that time he was hired
by his alma mater as a professor of English. Quickly he achieved recognition as a gifted
and inspiring teacher. For the next two decades, Ridpath developed courses in English,
"great works" literature, history, and political science. He also facilitated the endowment
of Indiana Asbury University and its renaming, for its benefactor, as (Washington D.)
De Pauw University.*

*Always an impressive and forceful personality, Ridpath produced such multi-vol-
ume works as his* Cyclopedia of Universal History *(1880-1885) and the* Great Races
of Mankind *(1884-1894). As editor-in-chief of the 25-volume* Ridpath Library of
Universal Literature *(1898), this educator shaped the reading of generations of Americans.
His look into the future proves as captivating as it is instructive.*

Among the greatest changes which the fifth Columbian year [1993] will discover will be the substitution of aluminum for iron, and that of sound for sight
in the work of learning. These things civilization demands and will find in the
Twentieth Century. Both of these substitutions imply a striking change in the
relations of man to the laws of his environment.

The progress of the human race has been marked and recorded at every stage
by the use of materials found in the earth. The present civilization of the world
is founded on iron. For nearly 8,000 years, iron has been the most important material
substance in the arts of life. We live in an age of iron. The whole present fabric is built almost exclusively on this coarse, strong metal. The age of iron marks
the first emergence of mankind into the conscious state.

Before the epoch of national consciousness, there had been two ages of stone. Barbarism has always had stone for its substance and symbol. In the intermediate stages of human life, the race advanced to copper and then to bronze. There was a brief copper age, and then a longer age of bronze. Finally came the age of iron. It has been the age of battle and power and conquest. Civilization has caught her hue and quality from that material substance to which she has owed her preservation.

We are not to suppose that the age of iron will last forever. Nothing lasts forever. All things obey the law of evolution and transformation. Just as stone and bronze have given place to iron, so shall iron give place to aluminum. The people will not call it "aluminium" or "aluminum," but "alum," for short.

There will be an age of alum surpassing all the previous ages of man's development. The age of power and conquest shall yield to an age of glory and enlightenment. Aluminum will be the shining symbol of that age. That beautiful, universal, and everlasting metal—constituting as it does so large a part of the earth's surface and body—will bear up the whole stupendous fabric of knowledge and progress that shall rise around our descendants in the closing decade of the Twentieth Century.

The world shall shine with the new luster of its principal metal. All things shall become whiter than silver. All the exterior aspects of life shall be burnished to brightness. The houses and cities of men, built of aluminum, shall flash in the rising sun with surpassing brilliance. All spires and walls, all gateways and porches, all bridges and temples, all moving enginery and far-off battlements shall blaze with a splendor befitting the new dawn of the ages to come.

The second great change from the fourth to the fifth Columbian year will be the substitution of sound for sight. It will be the restoration of the human ear to its rightful office as the organ of enlightenment and learning.

The sound wave is to be substituted for the light wave as the vehicle of all our best information and intercourse. The ear is to take the place of the eye for the interest and instruction of mankind. A most unnatural thing has happened in human development, for the life of all ages has been instructed by sound.

All mothers—from the mother bird to the mother woman—teach their offspring by sound, by utterance. But instead of continuing this natural process of instruction to the complete development of the mind, an abnormal method has been substituted. The youth at a certain age is led into a world of science and there dismissed to acquire, if he can, the painful use of meaningless hieroglyphics.

There he must study with the eye, learning the sense of crooked marks. These can, at most, signify no more than words.

Alas, how much of energy and life and thought have been wasted in the instruction of the mind by characters and symbols! How the eyes of mankind have been dimmed and eclipsed and the faculties overheated by this unnatural process of learning!

Man begins his acquirement of knowledge with words, and he ends with words. But an unnatural civilization has taught him to walk the greater part of his intellectual journey by means of arbitrary systems of writing and printing. The fifth Columbian year will see him untaught—a hard thing withal—and retaught on nature's plan of utterance.

Nature teaches by sound only. Artificiality writes a scrawl. Nature's book is a book of words. Man's book is still a book of signs and symbols. Nature's book utters itself to the ear, and man's book blinds the eyes and overheats the imagination. Nature's method is to teach by the ear and to save the sight for the discovery of place and beauty.

The fifth centennial of our discoverer will bring us the sound book in some form, and with that the intellectual equipoise of mankind will begin to be restored. The use of the eye for the offices of learning, in place of the stronger ear, has destroyed the equilibrium of the human mind. That equilibrium must be restored. The mental diseases and unrest of our race are largely attributable to the over-excitement of the faculties through ages of seeing.

The age of hearing is to come with the Twentieth Century. That age will restore the balance. Memory, almost obliterated, will come again. The perceptions will cool. The imagination will become calm, and the eye itself will recover from the injuries of overstrain and regain its power and luster.

Man will see once more as the eagle sees and will know Shakespeare by heart. He will remember all knowledge and will see again, as of old, from Sicily to Carthage!

John W.
Noble

The Rich Trans-
Mississippi West

One of President Benjamin Harrison's most admirable appointments to his 1889 cabinet was John Willock Noble (1831-1912) as his Secretary of the Interior. An attorney with a degree from Yale (1851), Noble practiced in St. Louis and then Keokuk, Iowa— where he became a leader of the Iowa bar. He served with distinction in the 3rd Iowa Cavalry during the Civil War and then built a thriving practice in St. Louis.

Through the 1870s, Noble's practice expanded into the American West and Southwest, as he successfully represented large corporations and railroad interests. When appointed to Harrison's cabinet in 1889, Noble led a legislative campaign to provide adequately for Civil War veterans.

Noble's most significant achievement, however, was the addition of forest-reserve sections to the revised land laws of 1891. Harrison immediately used this authority to withdraw huge tracts of the public domain to establish national forests. Following his tenure, Noble returned to St. Louis, where he enjoyed a successful law practice until his death.

The most stupendous changes in the United States during the next 100 years are to come in the far West. A century hence, the world will see, in the plains and mountain region of North America, an empire such as the ancients never even dreamed of. All through that region, much of which is now arid and not populated, will be a population as dense as the Aztecs ever had in their palmiest days in Mexico and Central America. Irrigation is the magic wand which is to bring about these great changes.

Last summer I traveled much in the far West, and the effects of irrigation are indeed wonderful. Here runs a ditch skirted by a hedge. On one side is the desert, a barren plain, only sagebrush and cactus growing out of its parched soil. On the other side are waving fields of alfalfa, grain, vegetables, and other crops, rich and luxuriant. The alfalfa produces three crops in a year and is splendid food for sheep and cattle.

It needs no prophetic eye to see this region all subjected to irrigation and one of the greatest agricultural countries in the world. With agriculture and mining, manufacturing will follow. The market will constantly move nearer instead of getting farther away.

Vast sections of our country, now inhabited only by coyotes and roaming redskins, will become the seat of the empire of 100 years hence. I have no fear that America will grow too big. This republic is not going to get so large that it will fall to pieces of its own weight, nor will the people widely separated by distance suffer from a lack of heterogeneousness or common sympathy.

To me, one of the most wonderful things in the far West is the likeness of the people there to the people of the Atlantic seaboard. They are with us in thought, in speech, in feeling, in aspirations, and in patriotism.

Indeed they have more patriotism than we seem to have farther east. The nearer one gets to the Canadian border, the warmer appears the love of the United States, and the more eager our citizens to float the Stars and Stripes. Up in Montana, near the British line, I found American citizens who kept their flags flying day and night, so anxious were they to advertise their country and their loyalty to it.

Notwithstanding the vastness of our area and the immense distances between our far eastern and our far western possessions, every truly national thought appears to be known in one place as quickly as in the other. What some one has happily called "thought waves" go over this country with astonishing rapidity. The habits of the people are substantially the same—the forms of speech, the idioms, even the slang. We are indeed one.

If this is true now with our present methods of communication, how much truer will it be 100 years hence, when to the mail, and the telegraph, and the railway, and the stagecoach are added postal telegraphy, electric railways, long-distance and short-distance telephoning as cheap and common as post routes, and heaven knows what other inventions for facilitating and cheapening communication and transportation?

Go into the patent office, which is a part of this great bureau [the Department of the Interior], and see what we have done in 100 years. With that before him, no man dare set a limit as to what may be done in the next 100 years.

As our country grows in both area and population, the means of communication will become more and more perfect, and Lower California and faraway Alaska will be as near to Massachusetts, New York, and Ohio in thought and sympathy as people of adjoining states or communities are to each other. But for these means of quick, cheap, and easy communication, preserving heterogeneousness among the people and maintaining sympathy and understanding between them, the future of this great republic would not be as bright as it is.

One hundred years hence, these United States will be an empire such as the world never before saw, and such as will exist nowhere else upon the globe. In my opinion, the richest part of it, and a section fully as populous as the East, will be in the region beyond the Mississippi River.

ELECTRICAL BUILDING

H. Walter
Webb

A Train Running
100 Miles An Hour

The career of Henry Walter Webb (1852-1900) offers an example of extreme dedication to his chosen profession of corporate management. In the end, that dedication compromised his health, and he died in the prime of life.

Webb was born the younger son of General James Watson Webb, into a leading New York City family. He was educated at private schools and at the School of Mines at Columbia University. He graduated from the Columbia Law School in 1878. Webb practiced law privately in New York City until 1882, when he joined the banking and brokerage firm of W. S. Webb and Company. Webb early displayed the abilities of a born manager, and the Vanderbilt railroad conglomerate hired him as a vice-president in its Wagner Palace Car Company in 1886.

Webb rose rapidly in the Vanderbilt corporate structure, and by 1890 had become a vice president in the New York Central Railway Company. In the absence of his superiors, the 38-year-old attorney assumed the corporate responsibility for breaking the 1890 Knights of Labor strike involving 5,000 railway workers—but the situation took its toll on his health. Recognized as a corporate leader with a brilliant future, Webb fought failing health through the 1890s and died in 1900, at the age of 48.

It is not easy to make any positive predictions about the increase in railway speed, or at least to put a limit upon the possibility of swift travel in the next century. Yet it is safe to make some approximate suggestions, based upon judgments that come from the experience of today.

A few years ago an express speed of 35 miles an hour was regarded as fast travel. Today there are a number of trains which make regular runs of between 40 and 50 miles an hour. And there is one train running from New York to Buffalo on the New York Central, a distance of 444 miles, at an average speed of about

53 miles an hour. This same train has made the run once at an average of just less than a mile a minute, and it frequently attains a speed of as much as 70 or 75 miles per hour.

This experience, which is comparatively recent, has convinced me that we are still much under the limit of what may be expected by travelers in the Twentieth Century. I expect to see, even before the Twentieth Century, trains running regularly at an average of 60 miles an hour.

And I have no doubt at all that, early in the next century, there will be a number of trains on some of the greater roads whose schedule time will call for as much as 100 miles an hour. I have no doubt that a traveler early in the next century will be able to get his breakfast in New York City and his evening dinner in Chicago.

We have already learned how to construct locomotives which are capable of making 90 miles and more an hour. And we have learned how best to utilize their enormous powers.

Given the perfect locomotive—and we have very nearly secured the perfect machine of this sort—we need only 3 or 4 other conditions. There must be a perfectly constructed track and roadbed. It must have inappreciable grades and very slight curves. And it must be so made as to be elastic and yet withstand easily the strain caused by high speed. Finally, we must have a perfect signal system. That I am sure will be developed.

The block system of today is sufficiently thorough to make the high rates of speed attained by trains on my own road, for instance, possible. There should be no grade crossing, as these eat up time dreadfully sometimes; passenger cars must be light, but very strong; the number of these cars must be limited on a high-speed train. We need the best coal and, of course, highly trained employees. With these conditions—and they are sure to be obtained early in the next century—I feel safe in saying that regularly scheduled daily trains running 100 miles an hour will be advertised by many of the railway companies.

The question of safety and of popularity will be no more considered than are the same questions when a person enters an ordinary express train of the present time. With the conditions that I have described above, a train running 100 miles an hour is just as safe as one running 40 miles an hour. In either case, if an accident happens, it is likely to prove disastrous.

The tendency of the time is toward rapid travel. It has already been discovered that these fastest trains are not an experiment, but are put on the roads in response to a public demand.

Charles
Foster

Electrical Power Will Be Universal

Charlie Foster (1828-1904) was born and raised in frontier Ohio, where he learned the family dry-goods business and became its manager at 19 years of age. Foster gradually expanded his commercial enterprises until he had amassed a substantial fortune in the banking and petroleum industries.

Charlie—a man of medium height, compact figure, genial face, and affable manners— successfully ran as a Republican for Congress in 1870-1878. Between 1880 and 1884, he served as Governor of Ohio, and gained acclaim for bringing business efficiency to state government.

President Benjamin Harrison named Foster his Secretary of the Treasury in 1891, at the height of the controversy over a national monetary policy. Foster favored international bimetallism, but opposed domestic free coinage. His positions produced many personal enemies across the country. When Harrison's term expired, Foster returned to Ohio, where he resumed his active business life—always characterized by a calculated, conservative approach to investment.

One hundred years from now, the people of the United States will be traveling at a rate of 100 miles an hour—on electrical railways. While traveling in the West a few months ago, I read a newspaper advertisement for a company that has projected an electric railway from Chicago to St. Louis. As I understand it, they are going ahead in a businesslike way, making contracts for construction— since they already have passed through the experimental stage and reached the plane of reality and commercial certainty. Their expectation is to make the journey from Chicago to St. Louis in 2½ hours, or at a rate of 100 miles an hour.

It occurred to me then that these men must know what they are about. And

I realized further that, if a 100 miles an hour can be realized with safety and economy in this century, it is not too much to say that 50 per cent greater speed—or possibly 100 percent—will be reached 100 years hence. Still, to be conservative and within the limits of the probable, I will estimate that in the year 1993 it will be a common thing to travel from New York to Chicago in 7 or 8 hours.

I remember also reading a short time ago, in one of [transportation expert] Walter Wellman's letters, that Thomas A. Edison, the greatest genius of this century, says that electricity is terrestrial magnetism and that the universe is full of it. According to Edison, the present system of producing electricity by friction is very expensive, compared with what may be done by simpler processes. Edison believes electricity may be pumped out of the earth, or the sea, or the air, just as water is pumped out of a stream. The only thing necessary now is to find the form of pump that will do the trick.

This, I understand, Edison is now looking for and experimenting on. If we may estimate his future accomplishment by what he has already done, he will succeed. He will find the pump that will extract electricity or terrestrial magnetism (or whatever it is) from the earth at a cost so low as to make electricity the universal power.

Imagine the revolution that will come in all civilization, if Edison or someone else succeeds in doing this. Given electricity at one-tenth the present cost, electrical power will become universal. Steam and all other sorts of power will be displaced.

With invention stimulated (as it will be) by the extraordinary cheapness of the new power, what may we not expect in the way of rapid transit, household conveniences, electrical carriages to take the place of horses, elevators in business and private houses, and all sorts of machinery?

If this theory of Edison proves to be correct, and the electrical experts are not mistaken in their plans for rapid travel, the next 100 years will develop changes more stupendous than have been shown by the last 100 years—in which pretty nearly every useful thing there is in the world has been invented.

I cannot rid myself of the belief that we are on the eve of an industrial revolution as a result of electrical research and experiment. And I take much comfort from the reflection that the people of the United States are likely to be the first to feel the good effect of the new dispensation. It will be the destiny of the American people to lead the nations on to a more perfect—and as yet undreamed of—civilization.

Elijah W.
Halford

White House
Will Be Enlarged

Born in England, Elijah W. Halford (1843-1938) arrived in Ohio with his family in 1848. He received a common-school education in Hamilton but, when his father died, he apprenticed (1857) as a "printer's devil" in the Hamilton (Ohio) Intelligencer. During the Civil War, Elijah worked for the Indianapolis Journal, *rising to journeyman printer, reporter, city editor, and editor-in-chief.*

In 1872 Halford founded and published the Chicago Inter-Ocean, *but returned to the* Journal *after two years. Into the 1880s, he served as the Indiana correspondent for the* New York Times, *the* Chicago Tribune, *the* Philadelphia Record, *the* St. Louis Democrat, *and the* Boston Herald. *As editor of the* Journal, *Halford published some of the earliest poems of James Whitcomb Riley and became one of the staunchest supporters of Indiana attorney and politician Benjamin Harrison.*

When Harrison became President in 1888, he appointed Halford his personal secretary. For four years, he served as "a useful and industrious lieutenant" in the White House. In 1893 Harrison appointed him a U.S. Army paymaster, with the rank of major. He distinguished himself in the paymaster's corps until required by age to retire in 1907.

Thereafter Elijah Halford engaged in volunteer work with the Methodist Episcopal Church and the Young Men's Christian Association in New Jersey. Halford deservedly gained a lifelong reputation as an efficient, reliable, and perceptive worker—all characteristics that recommended him to President Harrison.

Halford's comments on White House construction would prove prescient. Based on plans instigated by Mrs. Benjamin Harrison, the basic structure was renovated and an Executive (West) Wing added in 1902. That wing then was expanded (1909), and a third story was constructed in 1927. Following a 1929 fire, the West Wing received further renovation; the East Wing was built in 1942. More recently (1948-1952), under President Harry Truman, the entire White House was remodeled. Thus, Halford correctly predicted the pattern of simply expanding, modifying, strengthening, and remodeling the core White House structure of the early 1890s.

In the Executive Mansion of 100 years hence, I think I can see the present building as the central part. There is no doubt that this building will soon have to be enlarged. There is not room enough in it for the family, for the office of the President, and for the social entertainments or public levees which tradition requires the President to give. But I do not think the people will ever consent to the destruction of this house. Too many memories cling about it; too many of the great men and great events of the country's history have been associated with it.

Since I have been here, I have often wondered at the skill with which our forefathers built this mansion. One hundred years have passed since its foundations were started—the cornerstone of the White House was laid a century ago, the 14th day of October. And it is a good, serviceable, and comfortable house still. Its only deficiency is in the matter of room. It is stately, elegant, impressive.

In its enlargement, I think some such plan as that suggested by the late Mrs. Harrison will be followed—preservation of the present structure and a throwing out of wings on either side. That would give room for the living apartments of the President's family, for the public offices, and for the ceremonial or social functions which must take place in the President's house.

So the White House of the future will be simply the White House of the present, enlarged. I do not believe it will ever be found desirable to separate the President's residence from his office.

My four years' experience here has convinced me, moreover, that in the future the private secretary to the President and his family should also be provided with living apartments in the Executive Mansion. The President of the United States finds it necessary to work nearly all the time, and when he works he wants his private secretary close at hand. This means the night as well as the day.

Probably more than half the evenings of the last four years I have spent in my office, busy either with my own work or standing ready to assist the President. To do this I have had to leave my own home night after night, often at much inconvenience. The private secretary should have his home in a part of the Executive Mansion set apart for his use. And this necessity should be recognized in the enlargement of the house and should be made a part of the law under which the mansion is recreated.

One hundred years hence, I think the President of the United States will have much less work on his hands than he has now—though the country will be twice as great and the government correspondingly larger. For long before that time Presidents will cease to give personal consideration to a myriad of matters which now consume their time and their energies. The President of the future will not, in my opinion, pay any attention to minor appointments.

Every government post, aside from cabinet ministers, foreign ministers, a few bureau officers, and perhaps a score or so of the most important administrative offices, will be filled by heads of departments without so much as consultation with the President. Under the present system, four-fifths of the President's time is taken with these minor appointments. He is perplexed, annoyed, worn out by them. His energies are so sapped that it is only by tremendous sacrifice of comfort and strength that he is able to give thought and study to the important and serious matters of state demanding his attention.

Mr. [Secretary of State James G.] Blaine said to me a year or two ago that he believed the day was soon coming when a President would not permit himself to be bothered about postmasters, collectors, and consuls—any more than a railway president would spend his time hiring brakemen and track repairers. My observation in the White House has been that some such change in administrative methods is not only desirable, but absolutely necessary in the near future.

CASINO AND PIER.

COPYRIGHT 1891.
THE WINTERS ART LITHO CO., CHICA

Felix L.
Oswald

National Population Under 300 Million

Born in Namur, Belgium, Felix Leopold Oswald (1845-1906) graduated from Brussels University (1865) and prepared as a physician at Gottingen and Heidelberg. While still a young man, however, he turned to natural history. Oswald spent his life travelling the world, writing popular articles and books about his experiences and observations—for French and British, as well as American, publications.

This naturalist's most widely read books include Summerland Sketches; Or Rambles in the Backwoods of Mexico and Central America *(1880),* Zoological Sketches *(1883), and* The Bible of Nature; Or, A Contribution to the Religion of the Future *(1888). In the early 1890s, Oswald enjoyed one of the most extensive international readerships in the popular field of natural history. He died in Grand Rapids, Michigan, in 1906.*

A few years ago, Mr. [British Prime Minister William E.] Gladstone favored the American public with the prediction that, in A.D. 2000, the United States would have 600,000,000 inhabitants. He based his calculation on the fact that, in the course of the last century, the population of our republic had increased 1,200 per cent.

He might as well have inferred that a pine tree on its twentieth birthday would be a mile high, because in the first 10 years of its existence it had grown from an inch to a height of 12 yards.

In some of the eastern states, the rate of progress has even now fallen to one-third of its initial velocity. And it will undergo an additional reduction as the average density of population approaches that of the trans-Atlantic hives of industry.

It is true that the delta of the Mississippi River is more fertile than the richest bottomlands of the lower Danube. On the other hand, it is equally certain that the desolation of our western alkali deserts is unparalleled in the dreariest steppes of eastern Russia. Thus, drawing the balance of probabilities, there is no reason to believe that in 1993 the population of our present national territory will exceed 300,000,000.

Politically our federation of states will, by that time, comprise Canada and probably Mexico to the Isthmus of Tehuantepec [southeast of Mexico City and southwest of the Yucatan Peninsula).

This isthmus, before the end of the next three decades, will be crossed by a ship railway. The center of population will before long change its westward line of progress to the southwest and south. The climatic superiority of the southern uplands and the unrivaled wealth of their natural resources will ultimately turn the scales against every combination of prejudice.

Cotton will be spun where it grows, sleepy old country towns will be roused by the scream of the locomotive, and the terrace lands from the Ohio to the upper Rio Grande will be covered with orchards and villas. The 34th parallel will cross the center of that garden region, and it is not improbable that some industrial emporium of the "Piedmont country"—perhaps Birmingham, Alabama—will become the great city of the future.

Before the middle of the Twentieth Century, the increasing frequency of summer droughts will confront the farms of our middle states with the alternative of ruin or forest culture. The reckless destruction of woodlands has never failed to make the summer drier and warmer and the winter floods more destructive. But Anglo-American common sense will find means to arrest the progress of an evil that has turned the Eden of western Asia into a desert and has reduced the productive area of our planet one-third. Every country road will be lined with shade trees.

Forest reservations will comprise the upper ridges of all our east American mountain ranges, and large areas of the arid West will be redeemed by a multitude of orchard farms. For there is no doubt that the exigencies of overpopulation will eventually suggest the substitution of perennial for annual food plants.

Breadstuffs, as well as sugar and vegetable oils, will to a large extent be derived from trees that enrich the soil with their fertilizing leaves. These trees will outlive their cultivators, whose labor they will limit to the pleasant work of the harvest month. They also will protect him against the worst plague of the plains by affording shelter to myriads of insectivorous birds.

In the Atlantic states, competition for desirable tracts of real estate will, before long, grow fierce. Within the next 30 years events will prove that, while the risk of a religious war has been greatly overrated, the danger of a war of races has been quite as much underrated. The progress of education is gradually assimilating the intelligent classes of all creeds—but race instincts are less transient than dogmas, and the negro problem will yet loom up as the black specter of the North American continent.

North of the Tennessee River, Sambo Africanus will vanish as soon as the increase of population brings him into serious competition with European immigrants. Yet there are regions where climatic conditions favor the chance of his survival. On the Rio Grande, the aborigines and Ethiopians may coalesce against the north. Caucasian races and the struggle for supremacy will involve frequent appeals to the arbitrament of force.

To conclude with a few miscellaneous predictions:

—The problem of aerial investigation will be solved within the next 20 years.

—Transcontinental mails will be forwarded by means of pneumatic tubes.

—The perils of ocean navigation will be greatly lessened by the introduction of companion steamers, starting pairwise and maintaining communication by a system of fog bells and electric refractors.

—In 1993 millions of dwelling houses will be artificially cooled in summer, as they are now heated in winter.

W. A.
Peffer

Men Will Grow Wiser, Better, And Purer

Senator William Alfred Peffer (1831-1912), elected as a Populist from Kansas, was born and schooled in Pennsylvania. A school teacher at 15, he joined the California gold rush in 1850. Peffer moved to Indiana (1853), Missouri (1859), and Illinois (1862) before enlisting in the Union Army. He studied law during the Civil War and was admitted to the Tennessee bar in 1865.

By 1870 Peffer had located in Kansas, where he practiced law and published newspapers in Fredonia, Coffeeville, and Topeka. His (Topeka) Kansas Farmer became the most influential farm journal in the state during the 1880s. He was elected to a single term in the U.S. Senate in 1890—where his floor speeches proved heavy, dry, and often contradictory. After running an unsuccessful gubernatorial campaign in Kansas (1898), Peffer produced numerous literary works. His staccato delivery is evident in these almost Edenic pronouncements.

With the record of the past to study, we have reasonable ground for believing that men will grow wiser, better, and purer in the years to come;

That our perception of human rights will be more acute, as the field of view grows wider and our vision becomes clearer through knowledge;

That the common weal will be the chief end of government, the ballot of the poor will be counted, and the popular will be law;

That women will share with men all the duties of citizenship, land tenure will be uniform, the dramshop extinct, war abolished, and the people sovereign.

We are many times deceived by what we see because we see so little. We wince and groan under the exactions of wealth combined, yet in combination lies the highest form of exertion. Self love is the greatest of civilizing forces, yet the trend of life is upward. In promoting the comfort of others, we find the richest sources of reward.

While private monopoly in manufactures, transportation, and banking has shown the power of organized avarice to rob labor and oppress the poor, the multiplicity of inventions, the variety of modes, and the expertness in application have wonderfully increased the efficiency of labor, diminished the cost of production and added much to the comforts of men. Steam and electricity have conquered space and time, commerce brings the nations together, and intelligence simplifies trade. Thought is taking from religion its repellent mysteries, and association demands an international tongue.

So far will we have gone in 1993 that all of North America will be under one government, managed by a council consisting of a few men. Our great lakes and rivers will pour their waters through numberless channels for easy carriage of heavy things. The people will own and manage all instruments of commerce, every means for supplying public needs, all sources of fuel supply, and all unused lands. Lines of traffic will be straightened and highways improved, speed increased, and safety accrued. Men will navigate the air, and smoke will be suppressed.

Motion will supply light, heat, and power, and there will be no waste of fuel. Money changers will be shorn of their power, for then money will be made of cheap and abundant material and limited to its proper uses. There will be no usury nor mortgages—the year of jubilee will have come. Large landed estates will have disappeared, and one acre of arable land will support one person.

Justice will be dealt to all alike, and taxation will be limited to natural sources of livelihood—as land and water. The time of daily toil will be shortened to four or five hours. All willing hands will be employed, and effort will be ease.

Onward and upward will move the multiplying millions of earth, impelled by individual selfishness to minister to one another's wants, till trade is free and men's leading ambition will be to serve one another. Then the nations will be one, strikes will be unknown, and poverty forgotten. Great private fortunes will become historic, for men will have learned the art of just distribution, and there will be enough for all.

Charles Augustus
Briggs

The Sunday Press: Permanent, Powerful

That Charles Augustus Briggs (1841-1913) would take the time to discuss his changing views on the Sunday press is illustrative of his eclectic thought and indefatigable energy. For, at this point in 1892, he was spending most of his time propounding a defense on the charge of heresy.

Briggs was born in New York City and took his college course at the University of Virginia. After two years at the Union Theological Seminary (1861-1863), he spent four years studying theology in Germany. In 1870 he sailed back to become the pastor of a Presbyterian church in New Jersey, and in 1874 he returned to Union Seminary as professor of Hebrew.

C. A. Briggs spent almost 40 years in teaching, writing, and scholarship at Union. A bibliography of his books and articles published two years before his death contains nearly 200 titles. Ultimately Briggs held Doctor of Divinity degrees from Princeton (1875), Edinburgh (1884), Williams (1894), and Glasgow (1901), as well as a Doctor of Letters from Oxford (1901).

In 1890 Dr. Briggs delivered an address at Union on the authority of the Holy Scriptures; it deeply offended a number of Presbyterian conservatives. Although he was acquitted of heresy by the Presbytery of New York in 1892, the General Assembly condemned him in 1893 and suspended him from the ministry. Briggs ultimately took orders in the Episcopal Church, where he remained a clergyman until his death. He always exhibited an extraordinarily fertile mind.

I would not chance comment on the results of what is called the higher criticism upon religious thought in the next century. However, I do believe that, before many years have passed, accurate scholarship, exhaustive research, and intelligent criticism will be welcomed as an aid—rather than a hindrance—to religious development.

Rather, I would comment on the power of the press—and particularly the Sunday press.

I have recently realized, more than I ever did before, what the power and the influence of the newspaper press are. I have found that its desire is to report great events in the religious (as well as other) fields of activity fully and with accuracy. And I have no doubt that this tendency will continue. If it does, the institution is to have greater influence in the future than in the past.

But I have been especially interested in the development of the Sunday press, which is comparatively recent. At first I was prejudiced against it, and I would not permit any reading of these Sunday newspapers. Whether it is regrettable or not, I now realize that the Sunday press is a permanent institution, that thousands of religious people recognize and approve it, and that it can be made a power for vast good.

My hope and belief is that, in the next century, it will be cultivated by persons of high character. For the Sunday press can be made one of the engines for the dissemination of religious and moral truths and information. And persons of such inclination can rely upon it for those things which they desire. Meanwhile its influence will reach in the direction of others who are not now of a religious disposition.

I think that good men, recognizing that the Sunday press has come to stay, will undertake to make it an influence for good—as unquestionably it can become. Its tendency is certainly in the right direction. For the Sunday press now contains matter suitable for the reading of those of moral and religious inclination. And there are sermons to be found in many of the news reports printed in these issues.

Jeremiah M.
Rusk

Agriculture Can
Meet All Demands

Even in an age of self-made men, Jeremiah M. Rusk (1830-1893) proved remarkable. With little formal education, Jeremiah ran his widowed mother's Ohio farm at the age of 16. He removed to Wisconsin in 1853 and quickly established himself as a tavernkeeper, stagecoach driver, and farmer; he soon became a partner in the Viroqua bank. His extraordinary activity, sound practical judgment, and personal popularity made his numerous business enterprises uncommonly successful. He was known affectionately as "Uncle Jerry."

Rusk's political accomplishments were equally outstanding. He served in local offices and then in the Wisconsin Legislature, prior to becoming an officer in the Union Army during the Civil War. After returning to Wisconsin, Rusk was elected to two terms as the state bank controller and then to three terms in Congress (1871-1877).

Elected Governor of Wisconsin in 1881, Jeremiah Rusk served for seven years—and he was considered presidential timber in 1888. He became Benjamin Harrison's choice as the very first Secretary of Agriculture (1889-1893). Rusk's service was noteworthy for his move to inspect all American meat exports (thus eradicating some cattle and swine diseases in the U.S.) and for popularizing American agriculture through the national press. Although relatively uneducated, Rusk developed a writing style that is clear, straightforward, and logical.

"Will our soil and methods of agriculture improve so as to provide food without difficulty for all our population in 1993?"

It would take the gift of prophecy to answer that inquiry and, though I bear a prophet's name and am a seventh son, I never found myself gifted in the prophetic line. I can give you my opinion as to the probable relative production of this country when all its available land is subject to tillage.

But who is going to tell me what our population will be in 1993? I see that a writer in a recent magazine estimates that it may be 1,000,000,000 in 1990. However, I cannot help thinking that, in making such an estimate, he has indulged a little too much in prophecy for ordinary men endowed with but the usual number of senses.

As to the possible productiveness of this country, I would not hesitate to affirm that not more than one-fourth of the land available for tillage in the United States is now under cultivation. Consequently—without any further improvements in agricultural methods and with no more care than is exercised at present—the mere extension of tillage to all the available land would multiply our production fourfold.

Now, I have already more than once expressed the conviction that the yield-per-acre of most of our staple crops could be increased by 50 per cent, simply as the result of better farming and the application of the best methods now available. Suppose this improvement to take place, and you have a sixfold increase of our present production.

Further, much of the land which remains to be brought under cultivation must be cultivated by means of irrigation or reclaimed by drainage. And we know that—when land is cultivated under the conditions necessary to make these lands available—the yield is greatly in excess of that which is cultivated by the ordinary methods.

All these factors must be taken into account in estimating our possible future production. And we have not yet touched upon what inventive genius and science may discover in the interest of greater production and diminished waste in the next 100 years. But, in the light of what these agencies have accomplished in the past 100 years—whether the population of this country 100 years hence will be a thousand million souls or not—I think I have said enough to relieve your mind of any anxiety. Your children or your children's children should not have to go hungry for want of sufficient productiveness of United States soil.

There is one thing more that you must remember: before our own people go hungry, we will stop exporting food products. And the average exports of the past year or two would feed quite a number of hungry young Americans.

As regards exporting food products: while no one can realize more than I do the importance of our export trade, I would of course rather see our own demand increase to the extent of consuming all we produce at home.

And this reminds me that there is a good deal of wild talk about shutting off completely all immigration from European countries. Discrimination as to the class of emigrants that we should welcome to our shores is all very well, but we must not forget that this country was built up by immigration very largely. And I for one shall never favor the exclusion of foreigners who come to this country with the honest intention of becoming American citizens and bettering their condition in life by honest labor.

Between you and me, when I hear people croaking about the possible dependence of the United States in the near future upon foreign countries for its food supply, I am inclined to use a slang expression, and admit that "they make me very, very tired."

Transportation Building

Thomas L.
James

Postage Reduced To One Cent

Thomas Lemuel James (1831-1916), as a former U.S. Postmaster General, could speak with authority on the topic of postal development. James had risen to prominence in New York State by printing a series of successful newspapers. During the Civil War he served as inspector of customs for the port of New York, and subsequently became its deputy collector (1870-1873). Appointed the postmaster of New York in 1873, James brought reform, thoroughness, dispatch, and efficiency to the office.

Although offered the position of Postmaster General several times, James did not accept it until 1881. In office for less than one year, he eliminated an annual deficit of $2 million and reduced the letter postage from three cents to two cents. James subsequently moved to Tenafly, New Jersey, and became an executive with the Lincoln National Bank and with the Metropolitan Life Insurance Company. His reputation for efficiency and practicality survived his death in 1916.

We must remember that it is only a quarter of a century since the railway post-office was established, less than that since free delivery in the largest cities was begun, and only 10 years since the postage was reduced from three cents to two cents. Then we can understand how rapidly the development of the great postal system of the United States has occurred.

The Twentieth Century is going to see a marvelous fruitage from the seeds which have been sown since our Civil War. The first of these harvests will be, I think, a delivery of mails in which the speed of the telegraph will be almost rivaled. I think that it is going to be possible for businessmen in New York City and Philadelphia to communicate with each other by mail as easily during business hours as the merchants of each city can with one another.

I think it is quite likely that it will be possible for the merchants of the Mississippi Valley to send a letter to their correspondents on the Atlantic Coast in the morning and receive an answer in time for business purposes on the following day—and possibly on the same day. I think it is quite likely that fast mails running from 60 to 75 miles an hour will be found upon all of the trunk lines.

In addition to this, I think that scientific and inventive genius is going to devise a system of mail carriage that will deliver mails perhaps at twice this speed. Distances are being cut down for passenger traffic, and the mails will follow rapidly the examples of high speed.

I think that, in the next century, it is going to be possible perhaps for every citizen of the United States to have his mail delivered by free carrier at his door. Already we have taken vast strides since the establishment of the carrier system. With the facilities for communication increased at the tremendous rate which now characterizes these movements, it ought to be possible in the next century for every citizen—no matter where he lives—to receive his mail at his doorstep and without cost.

The citizens who live in the next century are not going to pay two cents for a letter postage stamp. The price will be reduced to one cent, perhaps by the beginning of the next century. The government has never made, and does not want to make, money out of the postal service. It only wants the postal department to be self-sustaining and the people to get the benefit of the profits. With the enormous increase in business that is sure to come, the revenues of the government will, by and by, be sufficient to justify the reduction of letter postage to one cent.

Ocean postage is going to be reduced so that we are to have penny postage, or a two-cent stamp, to forward a letter to any part of Europe. The ocean mail service will be improved until it becomes as systematic and regular as is the postal service of today.

There is another thing which is sure to come in the next century, and that is postal savings banks. There will be objection to this from some quarters, but my impression is that the people are bound to make such use of the post-office department.

M. Quad

Man Wears Too Much Cloth

M. Quad was the pseudonym of author and humorist Charles Bertrand Lewis (1842-1924). In printing parlance, an "em-quad" is the largest single blank-space square in the typesetter's font—an allusion fully available to Lewis's readers. Born in Ohio, Lewis graduated from Michigan State Agricultural College. For several years he worked in smalltown newspaper print shops and then began a journalistic career with the Detroit Free Press (1869). He served as a political reporter, but rapidly gained recognition as a writer of descriptive and humorous sketches.

By 1893 M. Quad had become a nationally prominent humorist, writing for newspapers, magazines, dime-novel publishers, and the stage. By that time he had moved from Detroit to New York City, where he wrote a daily column for the New York World. Much in the style of Western humorists Artemus Ward, Mark Twain, Eugene Field, and Bill Nye, Lewis never quite attained their status. The most consistent characteristic of Lewis's style is self-effacement—apparent in this piece.

I regard the present date as the climax of fashion in dress. While it has taken several hundred years to work up to it, the decline will be far more rapid. Man has simply been goaded to a point of desperation, and a change is bound to occur. I have already given an order on the downward slide, and in a couple of weeks I shall appear as a pioneer in the new movement. We shall not only restore the dress of our great-grandfathers before we stop, but run the costumes of Adam and Eve a pretty close shave.

Man wears too much cloth, and that cloth is cut up into too many shapes. The 20,000,000 men of the United States are wearing an average of twenty buttons each, making 400,000,000 buttons for all, estimated to weigh 23,000,000 pounds.

Five buttons can be made to answer every purpose, even at this day. Fifty years hence [1943], the number will be reduced to two or three pieces of fishline, or tarred rope may be made to answer every purpose. My great-grandfather used horse nails in place of buttons, and I do not begin to be as rich, handsome, and healthy as he was.

Collars, cuffs, neckties, starched shirts, sleeve buttons, and underwear are of modern origin. The idea of the inventors was to keep down the population by making man kill his fellow man, and it has been a success. Darius, the great and wise king of Persia, never had a shirt in his seventy-two years of life, and I do not propose to set myself up as being a heap better man than old Darius. There is no record that George Washington ever even saw a suit of flannels, and yet he managed to wallop the British and hold down the White House to the general satisfaction of the country.

Not one of the Pilgrim fathers landed in this country with socks on his feet or collars and tails on his coat. Any artist who puts coattails on a Pilgrim father ought to be sent to jail for his ignorance. Those things were not only accounted as superfluous, but positively unhealthy. The coats were tailless and collarless, and one wooden button was considered all that was necessary. Are we any healthier than the Pilgrim fathers? Can we run faster, jump higher, or stow away more corned beef and cabbage at a dinner?

Hannibal never had a sock on his foot. He never saw a vest. Had a man come fooling around him with a starched shirt, there would have been a sudden death. Had he been told that the day would come when a civilized being would have to buy at least three two-shilling neckties per year to be in the swim, he would have called that man a liar and a horse thief. Am I a better man than Hannibal? Can I have the cheek to characterize him as a slop-shop dresser?

Woman will keep right on until every one of her suits costs a million dollars apiece, but man is bound to return to the simplicity of Biblical days. Sandals, a toga, and a cheap straw hat will replace the costumes now worn. Sandals will strike us as rather cool for January, and togas and straw hats will bother us some at first with a blizzard whooping around, but in time the change will give general satisfaction, and we will look back in contempt and disgust upon the costumes of today. My straw hat and sandals are finished, and my toga is to be sent home next week. How they will take along Broadway is more than I can tell, but some one must pioneer the way, and I shall fall—to be remembered and blessed.

Van Buren
Denslow

Society Governed
By Economic Laws

The life of Van Buren Denslow (1834-1902) illustrates the successful integration of careers in journalism, law, and economics. Born in Yonkers in 1834, Denslow received his schooling in Chicago, which culminated in his entry to the Illinois bar (1857). He then settled into a solid law practice in Chicago, while writing biographies of noted Union military leaders for sale during the Civil War. For a number of years, Denslow headed the Union School of Law, until it divided itself between the University of Chicago and Northwestern University.

Denslow continued practicing law while editing the Chicago Inter-Ocean *for several years during the 1870s. He also authored several works on social economics:* Modern Thinkers, Principally upon Social Science *(1880);* The Chinese Question *(1881);* Freedom in Trade *(1882);* The Logic of Protection *(1883). His crowning work appeared in 1888, entitled* The Principles of the Economic Philosophy of Society, Government, and Industry. *This work profoundly influenced American economic thinking in the 1890s and was reprinted in 1974.*

In the late 1880s, Denslow removed to New York City, where he quickly built a lucrative law practice through consulting. He continued writing for newspapers and national magazines, and he edited for Gunton's Magazine *after 1900. As an economic analyst, Denslow had few peers at the turn of the century.*

In 1993 there would be a population within the present area of the United States of 580,000,000—if it should double every 30 years. The actual figures would hardly fall below 400,000,000. This total would imply an immense progress:
— in the irrigation of our arid lands;
— in the cultivation of our mountains and sand plains;
— in the drainage of our lowlands;

—in the utilization for manure of the present waste of fertility through the sewage of our cities;

—in the restoration of soils and of forests;

—in seed selection and intense plant culture, so as greatly to increase the product per acre;

—and in the introduction from all parts of the world of new animals and plants and fishes for food.

The average crop of wheat per acre, where planted, will be likely to rise from the current 12 to 20 bushels per acre to 125 bushels per acre, if all ground intensively cultivated is equal. The size of food animals will increase by 10 or 20 per cent, and utensils and dwellings will be manufactured largely of pulps and cements, so as to utilize vegetation and stone in every stage of decay, waste, or unfitness.

So vast a population could hardly be held under one government, unless the principle of federation should be so extended as to leave a larger measure of home rule, or state's rights, or "local option" than would now seem possible. I also think, however, that the states of North and South America may be wise measures of Zollvereins [tariff or customs unions among states], reciprocity, currency union, arbitration, and subsidized lines of transit. These aspects may become so interlaced and affiliated that the distinction between American states not now in our Union and those which are in it will be lessened.

As to the world at large, it will be more clearly divided between four great languages and races: the German-Anglo-American, which is Protestant; the Celtic-Slavic-Tartar; the African; the Chinese. The several Latinized languages of western Europe—English, French, German, Spanish, and Italian—will have become more nearly or quite one language, by a process of constant reciprocal borrowing of new words and because of their Saxon-Roman blending.

The functions of government will be less coercive and more suggestive— i.e., they will relate less to the preservation of order and more to the promotion of pleasure, progress, and the diffusion of information and thought. They will imprison fewer felons and publish more statistics. The army, navy, and treasury will decline in relative importance, while the census, bureau of agriculture, and geological survey will contain the substance of the government's future work and the germs of its future expansion.

The distinction between state and private management will not be so definite as it now is, as very much state business will be open to the influence of private individuals—much as the national mails are now carried by private contract under the restraints of open competition. Most education currently is done by private enterprise through the press, and in our recent war [the Civil War] the most effective battle was fought by the *Monitor*, a private ship worked by private capital.

The railroads and telegraphs will, in the near future, be the field in which state and private management will most freely blend. The state will manage on behalf of the users, and the trustees representing private capital will manage on behalf of the creators of these ways.

Public means also will exist for cooling all dwellings in summer and warming them in winter, for irrigating all lands, and for supplying power implements and workmen for all industries. The capital invested in these endeavors will be a source of private income to individuals, while the mode of use and the rate of cost (or the tax for use) shall be largely state questions.

Experience has shown that gold and silver coin depend for their abundance, utility, and value upon the private industry of the miners and the effective demand of the commercial world. Governments, in coining, can do little more than to certify facts already existing. If any change in monetary methods shall occur, it will be to make the issue of both coined and paper money more palpably an affair of private industry and less one state control.

Intemperance in the use of liquors now results largely from the custom of the "treatment." Treating results from the fact that the laboring classes get their news concerning work, prices, and the means of living in the saloons. Saloons also are the only places where a worthless man's opinion can find a hearing and where a poor man can drive a bargain or cater for employment without paying intelligence-office fees or broker's fees. If other agencies can substitute some different sort of clearing house for the worthless man's opinions and some other kind of exchange for a poor man's labor, there will be less treating and less intemperance.

At present every introduction to a new acquaintance in a saloon must be ratified by the social glass, every bargain must be sealed by drinks, every negotiation be smoothed by whisky. Yet out of these encounters arise most of the acquaintances, bargains, and negotiations which help millions to earn their living. If temperance legislation undergoes any changes, it should be in two lines: the substitution of pure for deteriorated liquors, of light wines for high wines, of cheap liquors for dear liquors; the official sale of liquors instead of the taxed sale.

The confinement and punishment of criminals is mischievous to the criminal, wholly without reformatory tendencies, and of little and doubtful value to society as a deterrent force. Industry is the only reformer. And industry is more promoted by marriage, colonization, freedom, and success in life than by enforced solitude, compact dwellings, constraint, celibacy, and failure.

Freedom of divorce is a race element. It was strong in Greece, lacking in Rome, a privilege of the male sex only in Jewry, but of woman also in Germany. Its adjustment will depend on a species of local option which will vary as race and blood prescribe.

As to the accumulation of wealth: the ownership of all the forms of wealth which are in social use must increasingly become the basis of private fortunes. But the use or loan or enjoyment of all this social wealth must increasingly inure to the public.

So long as daily experience proves that society gets the use of every form of social wealth—i.e., wealth which is so invested as to earn an income, cheaply in proportion as its ownership is concentrated into few hands—so long will great corporations and vast business aggregations grow in power and numbers. Because only through these concentrations can individuals best grow in efficiency, freedom, and power to utilize their time, talents, and private wealth.

The laboring classes will become increasingly dependent upon those who direct their labor in channels. These channels must produce work that will confer the greatest value on society, that will thereby earn or win the highest compensation for the individual, and that will permit him the largest personal liberty of action.

The liberty of the laboring classes grows with the efficiency of the organization of labor. This organization holds or steers or directs their labor, while largely supplementing and reinforcing it with machinery. This work's economic utility to society is always measured by the wage or profit or reward it receives.

Hence labor becomes free in the degree that it is bound to serve the needs of other labor—whose efficient demand is measured by its own capacity to produce what others will consume and consume what others produce. Present facts supply us with the means of determining that our soils and methods of agriculture will be more productive per capita as our population increases, until it shall have reached at least thirty-fold its present number. In 1993 it will not have passed ten-fold.

Society will be governed more by economic laws and less by judge-made and legislative law.

Medicine will be perceived to be efficient to the degree that it has been successfully administered to the patient's ancestors, neighbors, family, and friends. That which has to be administered to himself, it will be perceived, is too feeble to reach the disease.

All theology will be conceded to be mythology. Whatever respect is now accorded to the former pagan religions of Greece, Rome, Egypt, Persia, and India will be accorded to Christianity—together with the higher merit of having absorbed and utilized all the others. But the world, in getting away from idolatry, will not become materialistic.

The world will recognize the wondrous mysteries which underlie all the supposed simplicities of the material universe. And the world will perceive, all the more profoundly, that it would be impossible for any heathen artificer to frame an idol of stone or brass without successfully imprisoning the Godhead in the image.

The principal change which will occur in American literature will be that there will be an American literature. There will even be American art, American novels (in addition to those of Harriet Beecher Stowe and Bret Harte), American drama above "The Danites" or "Blue Jeans," and American music beyond our plantation minstrelsy.

Educational methods will be so modified as to reveal a high and fine art in broiling a chicken—but will dismiss the senseless and soulless clatter of the piano to the limbo of the obsolete. In dress, men will again wear colors; they will dress the legs in tights, just as soon as they again have the legs to dress.

Trousers will be relegated to bookkeepers, barbers, pastry bakers, and cripples. In the degree that women own the property, they will dress plainly. The era of color in dress among women for three centuries past has been due to the fact that men held the purse. The dress of women simply certified male generosity. As women come to hold the purse and the estates, they will dress themselves more plainly. Men will then put on color and wear tights to please women.

Still, women will never largely control the coercive or military functions of government. But, as these functions subside in prominence and the attractive functions grow toward their maximum—i.e., as governments seek coercion less, and education, art, and dignity more—women will come to do more reigning. Cities will become great only as workshops. The poor as well as the rich of the cities will have country residences—since the transportation to and fro will be so minimized that to reside in the city will be needless.

Every home will be a clubhouse and the words "boarding house" will follow the word "tavern" into oblivion. The chief discoveries will consist in producing fire out of water, silver out of clay, strong and permanent buildings out of paper, a locomotive force out of gravity, diamonds out of charcoal—and in making it always possible (because profitable) for every intelligent person to travel. For servants you will simply touch the button, and they will be turned on or off at pleasure, like water or gas by the general office. The mere fact that one is a "servant" will give less indication than now that he is poor. He may be rich, yet serve.

The race will be handsomer, healthier, and happier. Its longevity will so increase that lives of 120 years will be as frequent as now are those of 90.

Our greatest city will be near the Rocky Mountains—probably Denver or Salt Lake City.

The most honored American now living will probably be [agnostic lecturer] Robert G. Ingersoll. For deep odium while one lives is the surest test of a man being far enough in advance of his time to be hated by his contemporaries and, therefore, revered by posterity.

Generally it is essential to the broadest and most popular worship that one's influence be spent to mold and modify religion, rather than philosophy, science, art, or government. Ingersoll in this regard stands with Luther, Calvin, Mohammed,

Jesus, Buddha, and Confucius—an infidel to the ancient faith and a molder of the coming faith. Seldom can the laurels be torn from the brow of a man who successfully defends the character of God against the blasphemous aspersions of the majority of his worshippers.

If Ingersoll shall be most honored by the multitude in 1993, it will not prevent Thomas A. Edison from being most honored by the scientific class.

MACHINERY HALL.

COPYRIGHT 1891.
THE WINTERS ART LITHO CO., C

Chauncey M.
Depew

Two-Party System
Remains Invigorating

The life of Chauncey Mitchell Depew (1834-1928) never deviated from a high social, political, and financial plane. The Depew family of Peekskill, Westchester County, New York, could offer Chauncey a private-school education and a degree from Yale (1856). He tied himself early to the fledgling Republican Party, and became a central legal counsel to the party during the Civil War. After the war, Depew joined the legal team of transportation-magnate Commodore Cornelius Vanderbilt and specialized in railroad acquisition and operation.

During the 1870s and 1880s, Depew became the director of several Eastern railroads and the president of the New York Central and Hudson River Railroad. In 1888 the New York State Republican party endorsed Depew for the presidency, and he received 99 votes at the national convention. Depew remained a significant figure in Republican politics and was elected to the U.S. Senate in 1899, where he served two terms. Always considered a witty, entertaining public speaker, Depew delivered a keynote address at the opening of the World's Columbian Exposition in Chicago in 1893.

You have asked me to discuss the probable relation of American political parties to the government and to one another in the Twentieth Century, but this is a complicated charge.

The issues will, of course, constantly change. New ones will arise. No man can tell exactly what form they will take. It is very evident that the Twentieth Century is to witness a continuance of the prodigious intellectual, commercial, and religious activity that has characterized the closing years of the Nineteenth Century. Social, economic, commercial, and especially business questions will be represented in party platforms.

There will be the shifting of individuals constantly from one party to the other. Yet I am satisfied that the essential differences which will distinguish the two great parties—and there never can be more than the two great parties in this country—will be precisely those which have distinguished American parties since the foundation of the government.

There will be one party which will be essentially what the Republican Party of today is and what its predecessor, the Whig Party, was. This party will contain, as its germ, the idea which was at the basis of the party which Alexander Hamilton created. It may be called the party which favors the paternal theory

of government—although that is not a strictly accurate description. It is that party which has faith in the power and in the duty of the national government to do all proper things for the development of the prosperity and happiness of the American people.

Those who think as I do will call it "the party of progress." It is the aggressive force in the national government. It takes a broad view of the powers and responsibilities of the government. It sees in the Constitution not only permission but also command to do those things which are essential for the general welfare of the people.

This underlying principle will influence the Republican Party's relation to all new questions—social, economic, and commercial—which may arise.

The other party will be essentially that one which was created by Thomas Jefferson. Incongruous elements may appear in the Democratic Party, but they will be overwhelmed by this mastering principle of the party, as they have been in the past. As its vital essence, it will embrace the logical and the healthy opposition principle to that contained in the other party.

The friction between these two parties will be conducive to the national health. Sometimes the pendulum will swing one way and sometimes the other. But, in the long run, the average representing the extreme view in neither party will dominate the destinies of the nation.

This is health. This is the harvest of a vigorous and strong government. The Democratic Party will insist upon curtailing, to as narrow limits as possible, the powers of the general government. It will be sought by those who believe that the government should do nothing which private enterprise or states and municipalities can do.

We have in this description the animating influences of the great political parties of the next century. I should regret to see any other party—representing any distinction as its vital principle than those which I have named—arise in this country.

I believe that the political life of the next century will be as exciting, as invigorating as it has been in this century. For this political life has enabled us—with the shifting of power from one party to another, back and forth—to advance as we have in a single century from an inconsiderable people to one of the great nations of the earth. Undoubtedly, in the Twentieth Century, the United States will take its place of destiny as pre-eminent among the governments of the world.

William Eleroy
Curtis

United States To Dominate The Hemisphere

The comments of William Eleroy Curtis (1850-1911) on the relationship of the United States to Central and South America reflect deep convictions held by the journalist, traveller, and internationalist. Following graduation from Western Reserve College in 1871, Curtis began a newspaper career that took him from Chicago to Washington, D.C., to the capitals of the world.

Appointed a special commissioner from the U.S. to the republics of Central and South America (1888), Curtis intimately understood their economics, politics, and societies. In 1889 he was named the first director of the Bureau of American Republics— subsequently called the Pan-American Union. He served as chief of the Latin American department for the World's Columbian Exposition in Chicago (1892-1893).

As a journalist, Curtis developed an innovative column format that provided daily comment on foreign affairs for readers of the Chicago Record. His expertise in the Americas brought him national prominence. A colleague noted, "Curtis is a most diligent, prolific, and brilliant newspaper writer; a great gatherer of facts, an excellent interviewer, and a close observer." He also believed strongly in the concept of Manifest Destiny—at a time when few questioned its validity.

The manifest destiny of the United States is to dominate the American hemisphere. This will be accomplished not by political intrigue, not by diplomatic negotiations, not by the force of arms, not by the annexation of territory, and not by the establishment of protectorates—but by the influence of example and by commercial relations.

The tie that will bind the American republics and colonies will by the tie of trade. And in 1993 American commerce, to a very large degree, will be confined to American waters.

There will be a railway between Buenos Aires and Chicago. Thus the remnant of that race whose misfortunes have made the history of Peru pathetic [the Incas] will contemplate the blessings of civil and religious liberty under the shadows of the Bartholdi Statue and the Washington Monument. There will be weekly voyages across the gulf which divides the southern coast of North America from the northern coasts of Central and South America. And the theory of Columbus concerning a western passage to the Indies will be realized by the construction of an isthmian canal.

The fabled El Dorado, which was sought so persistently for three centuries among the green jungles of the Orinoco and the Amazon, will be found in the bosom of the Andes. And the gold and silver of Bolivia and the diamonds of Brazil will be exchanged for the cotton of our southern section and the manufactured merchandise of our northern states.

As we must have the coffee, the sugar, and the other fruits of the tropic zones, so must those who raise them have the results of our mechanical industry and genius. The Creator intended there should be an exchange of products between the American continents. He distributed their natural resources so that their population can live in prosperity and contentment without an ounce of European or Asiatic merchandise.

The value of the commerce between the United States and the Latin American countries in 1870 was $170,904,000; in 1890, $289,826,000; in 1891, $332,926,000; and in 1892, $381,440,000. These figures show that the divine purpose is gradually becoming a fact.

Michael D.
Harter

Governing Least Governs Best

In the early 1890s, one either loved or hated Congressman Michael D. Harter (1846-1896). For this commercial and financial genius had deserted the policy of the Democratic party and become a champion of the single gold standard.

Harter was born in Canton, Ohio, to a merchant-banker. He was educated in local public schools, never attending college. Rather, he took his lessons from the real world of commerce. At the age of 20, he founded the Harter Bank in Canton—an enterprise destined for long-term stability and financial success.

At 21, he was selected by the owners of the Aultman and Taylor Company to build and manage an agricultural-machinery factory in Mansfield, Ohio. This business never showed an annual loss, but constantly turned a profit—due wholly to Harter's direction. During the 1870s and 1880s—in addition to supervising his Canton bank—Michael Harter founded and operated the Isaac Harter Milling Company at Fostoria. He built this company into one of the largest flour processors in Ohio.

Given his brilliant, logical mind, his forceful character, and his resonant public-speaking voice, Harter was destined to be drawn into Ohio politics. A lifelong Democrat, he was elected to the U.S. House of Representatives for two terms (1891-1895), at the very height of the national debate between advocates of a single gold standard and supporters of a dual gold-silver standard.

On this issue, Harter broke with the Democrats and led the successful movement to oppose the free coinage of silver. Congressional legislation to establish the single gold standard for U.S. currency derived largely from Harter's mind and mouth. Thus Senator Harter was well-qualified to address the role of government in American economic life.

I believe that in 1993 the government will, if possible, be more completely divorced from ownership in railroads and telegraphs than now. Long before that

faraway date, however, a conviction will be embraced by the governing classes, by the newspaper powers, and by those writers who are read and those speakers
who are listened to. They all will conclude that the less the government med-
dles with private affairs, the less it interferes with commercial enterprises, and
the more closely it confines itself to the few (but necessary) functions properly belonging to it, the better.

The doctrine that the government which
governs least governs best will, much earlier than
1993, be the unwritten but fundamental law.
Instead of enormously increasing our civil service
list—which government ownership of railroads
and telegraphs would necessitate—as the nation
grows, I believe it will constantly (but perhaps
slowly) decrease. Therefore, while the aggregate may be larger, the proportion of our people
so engaged will be smaller in 1993 than in 1893.

Of course I know the apparent present tendency toward centralization. But 100 years is
a long time, and this will give ample time for
all of the great experiments in this direction to
collapse. In 1993 the government will not take
the child at the cradle and rear him under public supervision and under official
control at the expense of the community. It will not feed and clothe him, by law
and under rule and regulation, nor bury him in a state cemetery and put an official headstone up for him. Rather, a wiser generation will interfere even less
with him and his occupations than now. Men will be left to work out their own
salvation, politically and morally, more than in 1893.

What is true in this direction will be true of business enterprises of all kinds.
The man who, in 1993, talks of the government buying and operating railroads
will be looked upon by the charitably disposed as a sort of Rip Van Winkle. The
more matter-of-fact critics will consider him an ignoramus; the scientific observers
will conclude he is suffering from a mild form of dementia.

John
McGovern

Chicago Itself Will Support 3 Million Souls

John McGovern (1850-1917) spoke with authority in 1892 on the future of Chicago, Illinois. McGovern had been raised by a printer after the death of his parents by cholera, and he began his journalistic career as a printer's assistant (1862) in Indiana. After a short stint in Michigan, McGovern removed to Chicago (1868), where he started as a typesetter at the Chicago Tribune *and ultimately became its night editor. From 1887 to 1889, McGovern was the chief editorial writer for the* Chicago Herald.

McGovern always dabbled in literature and, early in the 1890s, he left journalism for a literary career. He wrote in several forms—from dramas to moral essays to poetry to novels. All of his work shows his understanding of the public's taste in easy reading, sensational matter, and moral emphasis. Ever a loquacious booster of the City of Chicago, McGovern was known as the "grand old man" of the Chicago Press Club until his death in 1917.

What will be the size and status of Chicago in a century? First, let us suppose that we have no war, pestilence, or earthquake, and that the Mississippi Valley has counted 100 more harvests, has garnered 50 billion bushels of wheat, has produced 150 billion bushels of corn, and so on. Then let us assume that this quantity of fuel has been turned into human energy, and that men have all worked like slaves, as they now work, with the almost magical use of machinery. Finally, let us suppose that Chicago is in the center of it, the largest city in the valley. Is this not a stupendous thought?

It will depopulate London. And—as men have always migrated when necessary, either by war or friendly reception—such a history might find Chicago with 10,000,000 people. It might extend itself from Wisconsin to Indiana.

About 600,000 people came here to stay between January 1, 1889, and January 1, 1892. If you knew everyone 3 years ago, there are today 6 that you do not recognize to 8 that you do. With blocks of 16-story buildings rising in every direction, with 72,000 persons riding in the elevators of one structure in one day, what shall the prophet do but spread the pinions of his imagination and soar to empyreal heights?

This I think I know of Chicago—that it is the cheapest place to live if one will work. But perhaps the reason for the inexpensiveness of life here is the low state of municipal cleanliness. Purity is never a bargain. Filthy streets, black buildings, unswept gutters and walks, careless raiment—these matters unquestionably make life easier, just as a soiled child in an alley has a much happier life than little Lord Fauntleroy, and lives longer.

Chicago has a level site and Lake Michigan to drink from. It has all the railroad trains and all the lake craft due here at any time, within a week always. So I should think that Chicago would support 3,000,000 souls at least within 100 years.

Yet, if the wage system remains, the only one that human nature will tolerate, it appears probable that the town will be a Birmingham and not a Florence. The black pall of smoke that lowers upon Chicago annually, after the sun crosses Madison Street going south, can only increase. For each new tall building empties its additional tons-upon-tons into the skies.

We ought to like the age of progress, and we do. Nearly everybody in America has sat in a velvet chair, if only in a railroad car. There are getting to be so many fine things that the kings cannot use them all.

A Chicagoan of modest means was awakened the other night at 11 o'clock by a telegraph boy. The lad delivered an electric message for his hired girl, from another hired girl, concerning an engagement to meet the next Thursday out. He was forced to awaken the girl and convey the tidings orally—as she could not herself read the plainest print. This episode bespeaks the democracy of the times far louder than a congressman's oration.

Andrew H. Green

The Finest Municipal Development The World Has Ever Seen

Perhaps no one was better prepared to discuss the development of New York City than Andrew Haswell Green (1820-1903). Born and raised in Massachusetts, he came to New York in the early 1840s and began a legal career with staunch Democrat Samuel J. Tilden. For decades, Green engaged in municipal-betterment studies and programs. For example, he conceived and administered the parks and transportation systems on the northern end of Manhattan Island—with Central Park as the focus and the Metropolitan Museum of Art and the American Museum of Natural History strategically positioned.

After serving as Comptroller of New York City, Green embarked on a plan to consolidate adjacent municipalities with New York. The result was the incorporation (1898) of Queens, Kings, Richmond, and New York counties, including the Bronx, as the City of New York.

In recognition, admirers dubbed Andrew Green "the Father of Greater New York." His lifelong expertise in handling municipal politics and administrative machinations proved this title absolutely accurate.

The greatest city in America and the greatest city in the world in the Twentieth Century will be that comprised in the metropolitan district of New York.

Chicago will be the most gigantic of the internal cities of the United States—numbering in its population in the next century perhaps almost as many as Paris now has [ca. 3,200,000]. But the New York of 1993 will have more than 8,000,000 people.

Early in the next century, the consolidation of all that section which is now comprised in the metropolitan district under one municipality will, I think, have been accomplished. This will then bring more than 3,000,000 people under one municipal government. And when we remember that in this district 100 years ago less than 50,000 people lived, it is fair to infer from the natural law of growth that more than 8,000,000 will be in this district 100 years hence, all under one local government.

It is to be the finest municipal development the world has ever seen. I expect that some of the problems that now face municipalities will have been solved by this grand congregation of citizens. The finest churches, the most beautiful architecture, the most exquisite parks, the most beautiful drives will give comfort and delight to the people who live in this community in the next century.

There are to be reforms of municipal administration. And I do not say that the New York of the next century is going to be ideally perfect. But I do say that it passes the comprehension of men now living to conceive the majesty of this great city as it will be in the next century.

FISHERIES AND AQUARIUM

Thomas
Dixon, Jr.

Life Must Grow More And More Complex

In the early 1890s, Thomas Dixon, Jr. (1864-1946) was serving as the spellbinding minister of the 23rd Street Baptist Church in New York City and a popular lyceum lecturer. But these were just two of this remarkable man's careers. Prior to joining the ministry, he had received a law degree from the Greensboro (North Carolina) Law School, done graduate work in history and political science at Johns Hopkins, toured the East with a Shakespearean road company, and been elected to the North Carolina legislature.

Dixon's background left him a champion of the Ku Klux Klan and other conservative perspectives. He was an author of numerous historical novels, his The Clansman *(1905) proving the most successful—as it became the basis of D. W. Griffith's landmark film* The Birth of a Nation *(1915).*

Prior to 1920, Dixon formed his own film company in Los Angeles and produced several films based on his own novels. Initially Dixon supported Franklin D. Roosevelt (1932) and served as a special representative of the National Recovery Administration. He ended his diverse life, however, as a Republican-appointed court clerk in North Carolina.

As to the political and social condition of the United States and of the world in 1993, I do not believe there will be a crowned head of the civilized world at the close of the next century. I believe that democracy will reign triumphant to the farthest limits of civilization.

It seems to me certain that government must grow more complex, if we understand complexity to mean the multiplication of its functions. "The less government the better" is a motto of an infantile republic. It is out-of-date at least 100 years. By government our ancestors understood tyranny, kingship, a power outside of the people pressing upon them. We now understand government to mean the people governing themselves.

As life becomes necessarily complex, so government must keep pace with the development of life. Otherwise liberty will become, at last, a mockery. The conditions of our modern civilization are far more complex than the conditions that our ancestors met when they made the federal constitution. That Constitution is utterly inadequate to the demands of the present. It must be magnified and enlarged—either directly or indirectly, by amendment or interpretation—to meet the growing needs of the new life of the new century.

It is absolutely certain either that the railroads and telegraphs will be owned and managed by the state or that the railroads and telegraphs will own and manage the state.

The question of money and the mechanism of exchange will turn entirely upon the development of the social question, which will be pressed to a climax somewhere within the present century. The present basis of money is satisfactory neither to those who believe in social reform nor to those who belong to the conservative element in the present social regime.

Within the next century, the saloon is certain to be outlawed in America and, when it is driven from America, the progress of reform will sweep the earth. High license will be weighed in the balance and found wanting. When this high-license humbug is thoroughly tested, exposed, and proved to be a delusion and a snare, the good will unite in a thoroughgoing, radical, prohibitory law.

The punishment of criminals, it seems to me, will be based more and more upon the effort to reform rather than to inflict penalty. Capital punishment will be abolished. It has now already collapsed. We had 7,000 murders last year and less than 100 legal executions. The sentiment of the age is against it, and human life suffers in consequence. The only remedy seems to be to substitute life imprisonment and to make the execution of law a practical certainty upon the guilty.

Our divorce laws must become uniform not only in America. There must be, in the future, an international adjustment of the principle of the home life. All international law is founded on the monogamic group of society. If Mr. Deacon fails to secure a divorce in Paris, he proposes to apply to the courts of America, and vice versa. The man who is interested in such a procedure may change the base of operations. And this option must be denied him.

The tendency for the accumulation of wealth in a few hands must continue to increase—until overturned by a social revolution that will make such an increase an impossibility. That revolution is certain to be accomplished within less than 50 years.

Great corporations and vast business aggregations will continue to grow greater—until, in their overshadowing power, they dispute the authority of the state. Then, like the railroads and telegraphs, they will be absorbed by the state. This tendency is overwhelming. And there is, as yet developed, no countercurrent to interfere with its inevitable result. Dry-goods dealers add to their general-stores departments of groceries; they are running out of the market thousands of smaller dealers throughout the city.

It is only a question of time until this tendency toward centralization and absorption becomes universal in all industries. It can only end in the destruction of competition and in the establishment of a monopoly—and the state is the only power that has the right to run a monopoly. This tendency seems to make the nationalization of industry the certain goal of the future.

The condition of the laboring classes is certain to become more independent, as they are better educated and learn their rights and duties.

Our soil is capable of producing abundant food for the world in 1893. But the methods of agriculture must and will be improved—else the present population, with its natural increase, could not be sustained in 1993.

Within the next century, law will be simplified and brought within the range of the common people. As a result, the occupation of two-thirds of the lawyers will be destroyed. At present, law is a stupendous swindle. It is beyond the possibility of any mortal man—it matters not how transcendent his genius—to know what the law is in America. This has produced such confusion already that a revolution in law is inevitable.

Medicine will attain the dignity of a science, having passed through the period of preliminary experiment. Theology will become more simple and central in its practical aims. Traditionalism will die hard, but it will surely die.

American literature will tell the story of American life and will, therefore, be born within the next century.

The sphere of music in the church, throughout the world, will be enlarged to the blessing of the race. The drama must be born again or rot of its own corruption within the next century.

Education is certain to be broader and fuller. We must educate the whole man—the head, the hand, the heart. Especially must our methods be revolutionized, that men may be trained for their work in the industrial world.

Dress must conform more to common sense and less to idiotic whim.

Transportation in our great cities will be controlled by the cities themselves. Sanitary improvements will become a religious work.

Woman will attain her status of equality before the law.

The servant problem is a part of the great social problem. It can be solved only with the adjustment of society under truer conditions.

Inventions and discoveries in mechanics and industrial arts will themselves form, in their enlargement, the basis of the new society which will be evolved in the new century. Pneumatic transportation as well as aerial navigation seems to be certain within the next 25 years.

The race will be both handsomer and happier in 1993 than it now is.

The greatest city will be in America. Its location will be dependent upon the development of transit facilities. If the freight of the world through the next century must be moved over waterways, as at present, that city will be on the Atlantic Coast. If water transportation loses its importance, the great city of the world may be developed in the interior. This does not seem to be probable, however.

The American now living who will be most honored in 1993 is that man who is most abused by the men of his generation—and yet who lives the truth in the noblest and truest ways.

Elizabeth Akers
Allen

Changes I Wish Might Happen

Although she is infrequently read today, the general public recognized Elizabeth Chase Taylor Akers Allen (1832-1911) as one of its favorite household poets at the end of the Nineteenth Century. Born and schooled in Maine, Elizabeth Chase combined newspaper editing with poetry and became a regular contributor to the Atlantic Monthly *in her mid-twenties. Allen's famous poem, "Rock Me to Sleep, Mother" (1860), illustrates her combination of fertile fancy and sentimentality. During the 1890s, Elizabeth Allen resided with her third husband near Tuckahoe, New York. Here she wrote a number of popular works of poetry. Contemporary critics honored Allen for her ability to express emotions that ordinary people experience. That quality is exhibited also in her series of "wishes for the future."*

I have here your invitation to contribute to a "Chapter of Forecasts" concerning the next century. But, as the "mantelpiece of prophecy" has not fallen on me lately, I am afraid my "forecasts" would be—like those of most persons—only a series of wild conjectures not worth anybody's money. So I feel conscientiously obliged to decline the invitation, while I would thank you for the compliment.

It would take much more than 500 words to tell what changes I hope may happen, or rather wish might happen (for hope implies a possibility of fruition, while we may wish for the most improbable things) during the next 100 years. As a mere hint at the list, I will say I wish that before that time has passed the world will have learned not to give all its rewards to the selfish, the unscrupulous, the dishonest, and the self-asserting.

Further, it is my hope, by 1993:

—That politics will be understood to mean the science of pure and just government, and not the mere means of enriching base, unprincipled, incompetent, and corrupt men.

—That it will be possible for women to walk from house to house, in city or country, in safety; that girls may go to church or to school, or even take a harmless walk in the fields or woods, without danger of being waylaid and murdered by their "natural protectors."

—That the persons who chance to witness a crime will not conceal and hush it up through fear of being put in jail as witnesses, while the culprit goes free on bail.

—That the worth of human beings will not be reckoned by their bank accounts.

—That this country will cease to be the cesspool into which are drained the disease, criminality, and pauperism of all Europe.

—That mothers will no longer be hindered of their obvious right to their own dearly purchased children.

—That the newspapers, which consider it witty to assert that the principal ambition of women is to be married, will be obliged to record on the same page half a dozen instances where women have been deliberately murdered for refusing.

—That literary work, like other labor, will be valued for its merit and not for the fortunate circumstances, beauty, prominence, position, or self-assertion of those who produce it.

—That sin will be held equally sinful and punishable, whether committed by man or woman.

—That the theft of a few dollars (or, indeed, any amount of property) will not be reckoned and punished as a greater crime than the ruin of a dozen innocent women by a bigamist.

—That those lawyers will be peremptorily disbarred who deliberately try to cheat justice by protecting known and proved criminals from punishment.

—That all mature, rational, intelligent, and law-abiding persons will have an equal voice in forming and administering the laws which they must obey.

—That, in short, the world will be as different from what it is at present as can well be imagined.

—That conscientious industry will win competence and comfort.

—That respectable old age will be honored instead of condemned.

—That those who deserve love will have it.

—That worth will be valued instead of show.

—That health will be contagious, instead of disease.

These are a few of the things which I wish; I cannot say I hope for them, for I see no prospect or possibility of them—and I dare not undertake to prophesy.

Richard Harding
Davis

Please Excuse Me...

Born to a literary family in Philadelphia, Richard Harding Davis (1864-1916) ultimately exceeded in publication both his newspaper-editor father and his mother, one of the prominent female novelists of her generation. Davis attended both Lehigh University and Johns Hopkins, after which he embarked (1886) on a journalistic career that made him the most widely known reporter of his time. For the next 30 years, he wrote extensively for the New York Sun, the London Telegraph, Scribner's Magazine and Harper's Weekly.

Davis proved an exceedingly prolific writer. In addition to a multitude of books covering his periodical assignments around the world, he wrote more than a dozen collections of popular-fiction tales, seven best-selling novels, and 25 dramatic pieces. While critics agreed that he was always readable and always vivid in his descriptive passages, they scored him for his superficiality, his contemporaneous focus, and his tendencies to be sensational and startlingly dramatic.

Davis's most enduring work derived from his assignments as a war correspondent. For prominent New York and London newspapers and magazines, he covered six notable conflicts: the revolutionary movement in Cuba (1895); the Greco-Turkish War (1897); the Spanish-American War (1898); the Boer War (1899); the Russo-Japanese War (1904); the European/World War (1914). His on-the-scene recreation of detailed episodes within each conflict brought Davis deserved renown. It is perhaps his predilection for the immediate, for the newsworthy that prompts his "solemn declining."

Please excuse me from answering any of the questions you suggest. They are too solemn.

Moncure D.
Conway

A New Theology
Must Arise

*The perspectives and opinions of Moncure Daniel Conway (1832-1907) changed
frequently and radically through his life. This intellectual eclecticism produced, however, some particularly predictive insights into Twentieth-Century theology.*

*Born to a Methodist slave-holding family in Virginia, Conway graduated from Dickinson
College in Pennsylvania and then became a circuit-riding Methodist preacher in Maryland.
In 1853 he entered Harvard Divinity School and emerged a Unitarian. His first pastorate
was in Washington, D.C.—from which he was dismissed in 1856 for his strong anti-
slavery views.*

*While serving at the First Congregational Church of Cincinnati, Ohio, Conway
wrote for myriad magazines and newspapers. He also edited the acclaimed monthly
The Dial. Conway lectured on slavery in England during the Civil War and remained
to lead an ultra-liberal congregation in London.*

*From both the United States and England, Conway authored more than 70 books
and pamphlets on topics as diverse as oriental religions, demonology, and slavery. His
later writings were biographies of such personages as Thomas Paine, Nathaniel Hawthorne,
Thomas Carlyle, and Edmund Randolph. Conway's Autobiography discusses, somewhat
successfully, how his ancestry, temperament, and experiences dictated many of his radical
changes of opinion.*

The human mind, inspired by the heart, shapes in the future an ideal that
survives the decay of dogmas. He who disbelieves in the world's supernatural direction usually transfers it to some natural providence, which will cause right
and truth to triumph. Even the pessimist believes that, in a world organically
bad, his philosophy is an exception—and that, when it prevails (there is just good
enough in the world for that), things will be better.

Our modern optimism buds on an old tree. An oriental poet reminds us that, when thorns are green and tender, the camel may browse on them. But when they are old and hard, the same thorns tear the camel's lips. Consoling and nourishing at first was the ancient pious doctrine that men should regard their lot as divinely appointed and be contented therewith. But this doctrine hardened into the sanction of oppressions and thorns for those who tried to improve the lot of the poor. And if the present optimistic sentiments should pass from poetry to practice, benevolent effort must be chilled.

For why should we do work which "the process of the suns" is doing for us? If humanity is progressing by a dynamic destiny along providential or other purposed grooves, our reforming efforts are super-serviceable and must decline with the increase of knowledge. But what we witness is the unprecedented increase of reforming and humanitarian efforts. While it has become a heresy (even in cultured Christian circles) to believe in a devil, the insurrection of human hearts against the world's tares shows a deep belief that the tares are permitted by no providence. "An enemy hath done this."

This separation between heart and head—between practical and theoretical religion—is the pregnant phenomenon. The discovery of evolution has revealed that we are in a predatory and cruel world, while increasing refinement has made the human heart more sympathetic. The earth has become conscious of its agonies. Sectarian partitions, originated by extinct issues, yield before the humanitarian enthusiasm. This enthusiasm is grappling with evil as if it were Satanic—just as theology has reached the conclusion that Satan does not exist, and that "evil is good in the making."

Thus the only fervid and vital religion of our time—in its crusade against evils pronounced "providential" by theology—is left without any creed corresponding to its humanitarian zeal. Science has taken away its devil. Common sense has discredited a deity that permits evil while professedly hating it. And the religious affections can find no shelter under an unknowable that is necessarily unlovable.

A new theology must arise. Whatever traditional dogmas it may preserve, it will surrender those that imply divine sanction of Biblical cruelties and of the like in nature. Humanitarian religion is an incarnation like that which once led the suffering world to worship goodness and love on a cross, rather a loveless omnipotence.

The new "plan of salvation" means the humanization of the world, including its dogmas and deities. When religion and theology reunite, there will be born, I believe, some successor to the ancient Zoroastrian philosophy of a good mind contending with (and through man's co-operation steadily subduing) inorganic and unconscious forces of nature which it never created—and for whose obstructions to human development it is in nowise responsible.

MINES BUILDING.

George Alfred
Townsend

The United States:
A Humane and
Scientific Empire

The journalist and author George Alfred Townsend (1841-1914) moved imme-diately from a Philadelphia high school (1860) to the newspaper world, writing for the Philadelphia Inquirer *and then the* Press. *He built a reputation during the Civil War as a war correspondent for the* New York Herald *(1861-1862) and the* New York World *(1864-1865). His accounts of the final battles and of Abraham Lincoln's as-sassination gained him nationwide recognition.*

After settling in Washington, D.C., in 1868, Townsend began writing a daily column for the Chicago Tribune, *the* Cincinnati Daily Enquirer, *and ultimately a syndi-cate that included more than 100 newspapers. Over the signature "Gath," these columns commented fearlessly on politics, society, fashion, and human nature. They developed Townsend into one of the most important journalists of the Reconstruction era.*

Townsend wrote from New York City from 1880 to 1892, but then returned to Washington. In later life he concentrated on literature—although his prose work clearly dominated his poetry and drama. George Alfred Townsend, his admirers maintained, could write with knowledge on any subject!

The federalist founders of the republic of the United States include [John] Jay, [Alexander] Hamilton, and [George] Washington, as interpreted by [John] Marshall, [James] Kent, [John] Quincy Adams, [William Henry] Seward, and [Abra-ham] Lincoln. They remain, in our day, the spinal life and brain of our system—despite the decrepit, chaotic provincial states included within that system.

These provincial states pass more and more to the rear (and are labelled dem-agogues and confidence men), as rising generations see the superiority of our federal institutions and spirit. In proportion as the subsidiary states share this federal or national instinct do they rise to the success of the nation.

I apprehend that it will take another convulsion (and that probably not an extensive one—perhaps a foreign war) to permanently settle the supremacy of the nation in every uncriminal mind. The weakness of the federal government now is due to the states who contribute to it their representative caitiffs as senators, justices, and even presidents.

The last message of the governor of South Carolina, the most wayward of all our early provinces, shows the failure of an obstreperous state sovereignty. Here the people—though they disobey the federal laws of suffrage—refuse to pay their taxes, maintain their public schools, uphold their one university (the first one where free trade, rebellion, and secession were taught), or subdue their factional and social animosities.

Good citizens of such a state must inevitably turn toward the cordial and helpful federalism at Washington. Further—when we have a less mercenary newspaper press and can, for less income, tell the truth—the poorer and more ragged states will come in like the prodigal son. And they will say, "Father, I have sinned against heaven and in thy sight; make me one of thy hired servants."

The necessities of dull states and the good sense of great states—all bear toward raising and respecting the one federal fatherhood. It is this government that taxes while we sleep (so that we do not feel the rib taken from our body) and applies that subtraction to delightful taste and intercourse.

Out of the one public estate have come all these railways, school sections, new and great cities, irrigating works, mines, etc. Where the federal works are expensive, the state politicians make them so. Who would not rather trust the United States engineers than a state legislature, either for wisdom or virtue?

The faith heretofore lacking in the supreme legislature through local and press demagogy will, when restored, make honor at Washington the public standard.

Liberty has descended to us through timorous and excitable men like [Thomas] Jefferson, as a stockade surrounded by Indians. Liberty ought to be not the suspicion of mutual egotists, but the beautiful respect and harmony between man and his family.

Some elements simply must and will yield: the unequal civilization of the parts of our country; the assembling as tribes instead of as fellow countrymen; the law of life and property in one part, the law of spasm and force in another part; the long results of slavery; the nonpayment of taxes. Excessive wealth, for instance, ought to be taxed in its full proportion, but not more. For if you re-move the stimulus of wealth, America is nothing.

The church has become a nonentity, except as a dead pull-back on bold and noble thinking. Literature, until the other day, had no care from the lawmak-ing power. Science is doing well, but is taking fat tolls from its generation. Would

not a better interpretation of government than ours have bought the telephone
at the outset for a million dollars—instead of taxing every customer in two generations fifty dollars a year?

Europe is influencing us greatly, and that will last long and probably will
be for our good. What could we learn from North Carolina or Indiana that would
be better than what we could gain from European intercourse?

We must nourish our peasantry, including the 8,000,000 of our blacks, for
an empire without servants might almost be without homes or utensils. What
have these wretched states done to discipline the poor in the mechanic and household arts?

The farmers are without public spirit or they would have better roads and
conveniences. From the cities and the villa seats will come the immediate helps
to progress.

Individual life needs more liberty than dogma and fashion will accord. He
who confiscates my Sunday to serve his superstition tyrannizes over one-seventh
of my life.

When we become free indeed, it will not cost us so much to live, for fashion and church thrive upon our acquiescent slavery. The home, too, should be
free. The civil, and not the clerical, power should do all the marrying. These broken
homes are often the result of the mercenary and secret priest marrying the dis-
solute, the half grown, and the runaway to each other.

Temperance and legislation have little to do with each other. Liquors ought
to be inspected and adulterating brewers ought to wear stripes.

Woman's great triumph (and man's too) will be not to need the ballot often; she ballots alone and uninfluenced for a man. Perhaps the old maids might
be given the Australian ballot to widen the understanding of it.

Private societies usurping the law's functions in the name of morals are Spanish
inquisitions. Too often they are directed by men of hideously perverted animality.

The United States—not the Texas contrived interstate commission—ought
to be a strong power in our railways and ought to own the telegraphs. The world
is interested in our becoming not a Christian, so much as a humane and scientific,
empire. That government would have one hand secured on the people's will and
the other free to labor for their lasting welfare.

I hope that the most honored American in 1993 will be George Washington.

Kate
Field

All Depends
On Our Women

Mary Katherine Keemle Field (1838-1896) enjoyed a broad public following for her many reform campaigns. Born in St. Louis to theatrical parents, Kate was schooled in Boston and Europe—where she developed lasting friendships with such literati as Robert and Elizabeth Barrett Browning, Anthony and Frances Trollope, George Eliot, and Charlotte Cushman.

Field returned to the East Coast after the Civil War to continue her studies of art, music, and drama, and to write regular pieces for national magazines and metropolitan newspapers. In the 1870s Kate received mixed reviews for a series of stage roles in the U.S. and England.

As a newspaper correspondent, columnist, and travel-book author, Field proved a woman of exceptional, if eccentric, gifts. She championed such diverse causes as international copyright, the annexation of Hawaii, temperance, and the prohibition of Mormon polygamy. She also founded and endlessly promoted the futile Cooperative Dress Association. For the last five years of her life, Kate Field edited a periodical called Kate Field's Washington, a platform for this well-known iconoclast's preachings.

What American now living will be most honored in 1993?

Grover Cleveland, if he fulfills the expectations of his best friends. Never were the problems confronting this republic so great and so many as those which the next President of the United States must meet and answer. On these answers depends our salvation for many a year to come. Hence the necessity of a great and enlightened patriot in the White House. And hence such a verdict as I predict should Grover Cleveland prove himself to be the George Washington and Abraham Lincoln of this generation.

Where will be our greatest city?

In all probability Chicago. There will be wonderful cities in the West, none more beautiful and extensive than Salt Lake City. But unless all signs fail, Chicago will take precedence.

Will the race be happier, healthier, and handsomer than now?

All depends on our women. If they marry for love and not for convenience;

If they cultivate the inside of their heads as sed-  ulously as they now study fashion;

If they "go in" for sound bodies, such as nature intended that the mothers of the human race possess;

If they teach their children self-respect and respect for authority;

Then Americans of 1993 will regard their ancestors of 1893 as more than vulgar, ignorant heathens.

What is the future of the servant problem?

Again, all depends on women. When they know their own business and learn the meaning of Christianity, there will be no servant problem.

What is the future in dress?

Once more the question must be settled by women. Should American women do their own thinking in the next hundred years, they will not import their fashions, and they will wear nothing that interferes with a magnificent physical development. Trains will be reserved for the house; corsets and high heels will be sent to coventry; the waist line will be just below the bosom; and [mythical Greek maiden] Atalanta will live again.

Is the condition of the laboring class likely to become more or less dependent?

There has been a steady improvement in the condition of what is falsely called the "laboring class," as though no one worked except the manual laborer. I only hope that the brain worker will be as well paid in 1993 as will be the manual laborer, who is fast controlling the fates of this republic and reducing human capacity to a dead level of mediocrity. All men should be born free, but all men are not born equal, trades unions to the contrary. There always have been, as there always will be, leaders.

What is the future in temperance legislation?

So-called temperance legislation is a temporary aberration of well-meaning but narrow-minded men and women with whom sentimentality supplants reason, and who actually think morals are an affair of legislation. One hundred years hence, personal liberty will be more than a phrase. When it is a fact, sumptuary laws will be as impossible as witch-burning is now.

Nym Crinkle

A Better Humanity, A Closer Fraternity, A Broader Charity

"Nym Crinkle" stood as one of the pseudonyms of Andrew Carpenter Wheeler (1835-1903), a journalist, author, and critic from New York City. After graduation from high school (1854), Wheeler worked for the New York Times *before deciding to test his luck in the West. He sampled frontier life in Kansas and Iowa, and then he became (1859) a local editor of the* Milwaukee (Wisconsin) Sentinel. *During the Civil War, Wheeler served as a war correspondent for several Midwestern papers.*

Under a series of pseudonyms, Wheeler built a career of art criticism for the New York Leader, *the* New York World, *and the* New York Sun. *His reviews of literature, music, and drama gained a wide readership because of their caustic humor and broad-based information. Wheeler also contributed to periodicals and collaborated on several plays and melodramas, from which he derived a considerable income. Wheeler's personal interests ran from law, medicine, and theology to songwriting, painting, and applied religion. This eclectic trait is demonstrated by his essay on the future of the arts in America.*

What will be the state of literature and drama 100 years hence?

To keep the answer to this question out of the category of mere guesses on the one hand and to save it from the imputation of rash prediction on the other, it must be deduced from the indications of the present.

There is a feverish energy in every department of intellectual life just now that is symptomatic. Every person of fairly good education and of restless mind writes a book. As a rule, it is a superficial book. But it swells the bulk, and it indicates the cerebral unrest that is trying to express itself. We have arrived at a condition in which more books are printed than the world can read. This is true not only of books that are not worth reading, but it is true of the books that are.

All this I take to be the result of an intellectual affranchisement that is new. And it is the result of a dissemination of knowledge, instead of a concentration of culture. Everybody wants to say something. But it is slowly growing upon the world that everybody has not got something to say.

Therefore one may, even at this moment, detect the causes which will produce reaction. In 100 years there will not be so many books printed, but there will be more said. That seems to me to be inevitable. Movement is certainly in the direction of intellectual development. This implies that man reaches a condition individually and socially (if he progresses at all) in which he cares less about talking than about doing.

But, first, let us take the whole bulk of current literature—good, bad, and indifferent—and acknowledge that, as a mass it is more active than profound. There is, nevertheless, an observable tendency in it: it is measurably moving toward a *somewhat!* So, if we can get the direction and the ratio, we may reasonably measure its progress during the next century.

Now what is that tendency?

I do not see how any one can diligently investigate the current material without perceiving that its slow advance is toward a better humanity, a closer fraternity, a broader charity. These signs are unmistakable, even in its lighter veins of cynicism and persiflage.

Nine-tenths of all the imaginative writers are jibing at the wrongs of society. The other tenth are jibing at its political shortcomings. Of course they have ideals, against which they adjust the real. Some of these ideals are made of moonbeams; some are wildly impracticable; others are fantasies on Plato's notion or travesties of [Thomas] More's dream. But the incentive is a restless sense of imperfection and a growing consciousness of a central sun somewhere in the moral and intellectual universe which is pulling all things to it. When this is not a distinctly theistic feeling, it is a vague philosophic counterpart of it.

So far as this is a gain in unity and reasonableness, it is a permanent gain. I can conceive of no political or social disaster that will destroy it.

The philosopher who undertakes to survey this ground needs not be an extreme optimist to see that there is a distinct ethical gain in the aggregate of intellectual work. When it does not lead it reflects, in broken and uncertain gleams, the spirit of the age—and that spirit stands for a better solidarity and a nobler destiny for man.

Under all the factors that must influence the intellectual future, broader and deeper than any of them lies education. If you want to find out what the future man will say, you will have to ask, "What will he know?"

At this moment the whole educational energy of the country is centering itself on the want of an ethical basis of instruction. It is not alone the Catholic Church that objects to the system which makes smart men instead of good men. Some of the wisest of Protestant teachers have conceded that our public-school system is fatally deficient in the elemental teaching which develops the moral sense and makes honest citizens.

This protest, I take it, is another form of the reaction against the intense materialism of the time. But it is also a sign of intellectual development. No one who studies it can doubt that the education of our youth during the next 50 years will be in a measure freed from the mathematical restrictions of the present course.

We must recognize the fact that labor everywhere is insisting that more time to study and to rest shall be taken from toil, and add this to the fact that the studies promise to improve in the direction of ethics. Thus I do not see how we can avoid the conclusion that—barring some great and incalculable convulsion that would throw mankind backward 100 years—the coming intellectual workers will be less superficial, more thoroughly equipped for their work, of larger views and broader catholic spirit, with less creed in their religion and more of God and humanity. The encyclopedic man, who makes a show of knowing all things, will give way to the specialist, who makes an effort to know one thing and know it well.

The newspaper which has made a bold incursion into current literature has, with the stimulus of competition, overdone the matter. There is already a tendency to go to the review for expressions of opinion. We hear continually of the demoralization of the press, which means the popularization of the newspaper at the expense of conviction.

There is going to be a reaction in that field. There ought to be. And there undoubtedly will be, in New York or some other commercial and intellectual American center, a press which will express the convictions of the wisest minds in all departments of thought—irrespective of what a party or a corporation or an advertiser wants.

Such a paper whose opinions cannot be bought, whose convictions cannot be frightened, and whose good will cannot be cajoled will bring the power of the press up to the traditional standard. And its opinion will command the attention of the world. It is American just now to want the news. As the facilities for gathering it and disseminating it increase, the intelligent public will want something else. They will reflect as well as apprehend.

They will have more leisure to think. The present rate of headlong material activity cannot be kept up for another 100 years. Already a new class is multiplying, which is reaping the leisure that its fathers made possible with drudgery and heart failure. The continent is all explored and nearly all surveyed. There will scarcely be another Pike's Peak fever. While I am writing this, the statesmen of the country are asking themselves if it is not time to make laws which shall restrict—if they do not put a stop to—immigration.

In 100 years Denver will be as big as New York and in the center of a vast population. If the republic remains politically compact and does not fall apart at the Mississippi River, Canada will be either part of it or an independent sovereignty. And the northern shore of the Gulf of Mexico will be the Riviera of the western continent.

It is not possible to estimate the perpetuity and progress of the United States without feeling that its political majesty and its beneficent freedom will react upon the intellectual expression of the people. The solidarity, the general happiness of the nation, will find an outcome in nobler works of art and science.

In that 100 years, we will have matured our poet and found our Moliere or our Shakespeare. The gestation of genius is by centuries.

Of course I do not suppose that the incoming century will bring the millennium. We all know that progress often depends on disaster, as character depends on suffering, and no one can tell what upheavals are in store for us. History, on the whole, is very sad reading. And it teaches the lesson not of uninterrupted material prosperity, but of rise, decline, and fall.

But in our present rate of progress is much hope and some calculable signs. In 100 years the public will desire better reading, because it must reach a better plane of thinking. The germs of great universities will have matured their fruit by that time. The world will be in closer touch. Mercy will march with war and arbitration precede it. Somewhere the nation will have an intellectual capital with a national library and a national theater. It will have developed an art school of its own.

The ideal man and woman will have an opportunity to use all the plastic arts, and they will speak to us in literature and drama. The homes of the country will have been quadrupled—and it is the home that fixes the status of the theater. As we increase the enjoyments of the family circle, we lessen the attraction of the cheap public entertainments, which depend upon the hotels and the floating population.

We can see even now that sectarian barriers are crumbling. Men are climbing over the ecclesiastical fences to get nearer to each other. And they have found that, as they come together, they approach the eternal reason.

In 100 years, man will have learned the lesson of trusting his brother. And the nation which has drawn all peoples to it with a cosmic gravitation and lifted them with freedom and confidence will also have destroyed the prejudices of race and the animosities of sect.

Such a view presents the new solidarity of fraternity. But it is the old lesson which that first democrat dauntlessly proclaimed on Mars' hill.

John
Swinton

The Whirligig
Of Time

A journalist and social reformer, John Swinton (1829-1901) built a reputation as a man of unblemished integrity. Swinton was born in Scotland and moved with his family first to Canada and then (1852) to New York City. As a journeyman printer, he travelled in the South and Midwest, but returned to New York to study law and medicine. In 1860 he began a ten-year stint as chief of the editorial staff for the New York Times. Swinton subsequently (1875-1883) wrote editorials for the New York Sun.

John Swinton became deeply involved in both the labor and the social-reform movements. In 1874 he led one faction of the Tompkins Square demonstration, and he ran for the mayor of New York City on the Industrial-Political Party ticket. From 1883 to 1887, he published John Swinton's Paper, *a weekly labor journal of the highest quality. He also authored several pamphlets and a labor volume,* Striking for Life *(1894).*

As a writer, Swinton was truly distinguished. He demonstrated a rare sense of word values and prose clarity. "Both in vehement invective and in biting sarcasm, he was a master of the language of opprobrium." Despite his radicalism, John Swinton remained a fervently religious Scotch Calvinist—and a man of unblemished integrity.

When the old saw grinder said that "We can judge of the future only by the past," and he predicted that "The things which will be are the things which have been," I replied to him in the Hebrew language with the word "Amen!"

Well, then, suppose that the wiseacres of the Fifteenth Century, while hanging up these maxims, had judged of the future Sixteenth Century by the past Fourteenth Century. They would have concluded that the one must be even as the other had been. And it would be evident to us of this time that they did not foresee the consequences of the discovery of America, or of Gutenberg's invention, or of Luther's antipapal mutiny, or of the doom of Islam, or of the Renáissance.

So, again, what if the wiseacres who lived at the opening of the last century—when Louis XIV was king of France and William III was the sovereign of the British American colonies—believed that their century would leave things as they found them? It would now be evident to us who live at this time that they had not forecast the events of 1776 in this country, or those of 1793 in France, or many others that were on record before the year 1800.

And so, yet again, it is the case with the wiseacres who would have worked the old saw at the opening of our own Nineteenth Century. While judging the future by the past, they would not have any prevision of the transformations to be brought about during the century in South America, Asia, and Africa, or even such European countries as Germany and Italy.

I cannot foretell the course or the operations of the whirligig of time during the next 100 years. But I am disposed to surmise that the historian who in 1993 makes record thereof will have to get up a big book.

I guess that there will be great political and social changes in our country before the year 1993. And I suppose that these changes will be advantageous to the community at large. I guess that before the next century shall end:

—The functions and powers of our government will be greatly enlarged;

—Railroads, telegraphs, and many other things now held as private spoil will be public property;

—Law, medicine, and theology will be more reasonable than they now are;

—Inventions and discoveries will be greater than we have ever yet had;

—The welfare of mankind will be higher than it is in this age of confusion.

WOMANS BUILDING.

Erastus
Wiman

A New Field Opens—
The Canadian North

The observations of Erastus Wiman (1834-1904) on commercial cooperation between Canada and the United States arise from his Canadian background. Born in Ontario, he moved with his family to Toronto, where he became a printer, a reporter, and then the commercial editor of the Toronto Globe. He also edited the Montreal Trade Review before coming to New York City (1867) as an agent in R. G. Dun and Company's mercantile company.

Wiman served as a director of the Western Union Telegraph Company and was president of the Staten Island Rapid Transit Railway (1884). Perhaps his greatest feat was the construction of the Arthur Kill Bridge, between New Jersey and Staten Island— for this structure made more than ten miles of waterfront in New York harbor accessible to trunk railroads. For this accomplishment, Wiman gained the nickname "The King of Staten Island."

Erastus Wiman promoted continually the concept of a Zollverein (a tariff or customs union among states) for all countries of North and South America. Yet he was most adamant that reciprocal trade agreements between the United States and Canada be established, maintained, and enhanced.

Because there are children now living who will realize 50 years hence all the advantages that are likely to occur between now and then, it seems preferable to make a forecast of half a century, rather than of a whole century. There is something realizable, something within sight, in 50 years. Pushing the prospect away 100 years seems to make the vision too dim and distant for practical purposes.

Up to this period in the history of the United States its people have been busy in developing only that within its own borders. Ever-widening areas have given abundant opportunity, not only for the vast emigration that has reached these shores, but for the natural increase of population.

The development of natural resources so vast and varied have rendered employment constant and profitable. Enormous additions by emigration have provided ready-made customers on the one hand and abundant labor on the other.

Everything within the country itself has contributed to its own progress until now, at the closing years of its first century of progress, it has reached a condition at which all the world wonders.

But with the first 50 years of the new century these conditions will very materially change, so far as the enormous increase in population is concerned. If the population increases at the same relative rate in the next five decades as in the last 50 years, the number of people to be sustained on this continent will be between 150,000,000 and 200,000,000.

If the field of opportunity is beginning to be limited when the population is less than 65,000,000, what will be the limitations when the population reaches three times that amount? It is no extraordinary estimate to believe that 195,000,000 will need to find employment, need to be governed and, above all, need to be fed, before boys and girls now born will cease to live. The prospect is rather a startling one.

It is particularly so with regard to the shape that matters are taking as to trusts, combinations, and consolidations. If competition is to be eliminated, production regulated, and prices fixed by the few, the enormous increase in population will find conditions more extraordinary than ever anybody dreamed of.

What if, for instance, coal—one of the chief factors and forces in civilization—should be controlled by ten or a dozen men? That would compel the government to take possession of all the coal lands, to be sure of supply and a lack of interference. Equally so with oil, with sugar, and with the thousand other things now drifting into the control of a few.

But the tendency in this strange and rather dangerous direction is likely to be checked by the economic revolution recently witnessed in the [1892] presidential election. The change which is implied in the election of Mr. [Grover] Cleveland is that an effort will be made to build up a trade other than that which exists in the country itself. It would seem that this change comes at the most appropriate time. It also seems that revolutions resembling special providences come only when needed—and when needed their effects come to stay.

If the destiny of this country limited its operations exclusively to within its own borders, there would be precious little hope for the 200,000,000 that in 50 years are to be taken care of in this country. But—with the world open as a field, with taxation reduced to a minimum, without the need of a standing army, with abundant supply of raw material, and with food products cheaper than elsewhere in the world— it would seem that the destiny of the United States included the creation of a commerce with foreign lands. And this international trade would exceed that vast internal commerce which she has already created within her own limits.

The extent and magnitude of this internal trade almost exceeds human estimate. It is one of the most wonderful demonstrations of human progress the world has ever seen. Yet the foreign commerce of which the United States is capable is  destined to even exceed these enormous figures. And in that foreign commerce exists the hope of the future generations of this continent.

Hence the revolution which now impends in economic affairs is of great moment in the forecast of the next 50 years. First must be applied the genius of the people of this country, its inventive faculty, and the introduction of steam, machinery, and electricity. Then the forces that have chiefly contributed to the progress of the United States will be made as effective for the benefit of the whole world as they have been for this country itself.

There is no apparent limit, except the limit of the world itself, to the growth of wealth, to the augmentation of opportunity, and to the achievements of this American people. Fifty years hence boys now living will look back with wonderment at the narrowness of the comprehension of even great political parties, who sought to restrict the operations of the continent so vast in its forces to the development of trade within itself.

The growth of the commerce of Great Britain is the best illustration of what may occur in the United States in the next 50 years under changed conditions. The British islands, which are a mere speck upon the map of the world, levy tribute from every nation under the sun. This they do in spite of distance from supplies of raw material, with the necessity of the purchase of food products from distant climes, and in circumstances altogether disadvantageous, as compared with those existing in the United States.

By her commercial policy, Great Britain has regulated, up to this time, the commerce of the world. She holds the supremacy upon the seas by her great maritime wealth. By her accumulations of capital she has regulated the monetary affairs of the entire financial fabric of the earth. In the next 50 years, surely the United States can do more.

But it is not outside the continent alone that, in the next 50 years, so much will be achieved. Turning northward, a region exists similar to the United States in products. This land exceeds in area and riches those which have here been developed. A new field opens—not only for achievement within the region itself, but furnishing all the material essential for success abroad.

Thus, in the articles of food, limitations are already being reached with a population of 65,000,000. A population of 100,000,000 or 150,000,000 will beget the greatest anxiety. There are only two classes that produce food—the fisherman and the farmer. In the decade just closing, the cities (in which no food is produced) increased 60 per cent, while the farmer increased only 14 per cent. The fisherman showed no increase at all—rather diminishing in number and in extent of output. If the same ration of increase should continue, with the increased population referred to, it would be very soon seen that the question of food is to be one of the greatest importance within the next 50 years.

The bread which now sustains the population is from flour derived from the most northern states. These arable soils are being exhausted by constant cultivation, and yet the trend of the growth of wheat continues northward. Minnesota and Dakota furnish now three-fourths of the entire flour product of this country. In 15 years, it is alleged, the exporting of all food products, including provisions, will cease. This will be the result of the diminishing amount on the one hand and of the increased consumption by growth of population on the other.

Under such circumstances, the enormous wheat areas of the British possessions in North America are of great importance to this country. Not only will they have importance as a source of supply. But, by their occupancy through emigration and otherwise, they would create a vast market so accessible and so exclusive to the United States that nothing in its history would so benefit its trade.

Michigan, Wisconsin, and Minnesota have been contributory to the benefits of this country in absorption of goods on the one hand and their supply of food and raw material on the other. So will also the development of regions of equal area and equal richness within the British possessions.

The impending economic revolution, therefore, is as full of significance regarding the northern region of the continent as it is regarding the foreign trade. Without the drawing of a sword, the shedding of a drop of blood, or the expenditure of a single dollar, the area of the trade of the United States can thus be doubled. It needs only a single act of the legislatures at Washington and Ottawa to have the barrier broken down. Within just 5 years, the foundation can be laid for a progress on this continent, during the next 50 years, that will be measured only by that which has taken place south of its center during the last 50 years.

The field of opportunity for the next 50 years is that portion of the continent now unoccupied. The young men in our colleges and schools, when they come out, need the same chance that their predecessors have had. That chance is pretty well preempted.

The limitations in area in the United States have been reached. A "land hunger" has already set in—as shown in the tremendous rush for farms at the opening of every government reserve. It is impossible to get a new farm in Minnesota any more readily than it is in Pennsylvania without displacing a farmer. And, unless the people continue to herd in the cities, crowding the manufactories, or live one upon another, there must be room for expansion. Canada affords that room.

The maritime provinces—described by Governor [John Albion] Andrew of Massachusetts as "possessing greater wealth in minerals and agricultural possibilities than New York and Pennsylvania"—with a great coastline of fisheries added, offer great inducements for young men in the eastern states. The ability of these provinces to contribute raw material, which New England needs for the creation of a foreign trade, is as palpable as that warmth comes from the sun.

Equally so with the great manufacturing facilities and raw material in the province of Quebec. Further, there exists an enormous possible output of food products from the province of Ontario. And the minerals of Algoma [Ontario], that treasure box of the continent, invite the energy and capital of the American people to a degree that California never possessed.

These, however, are but the vestibule to the vast wheat fields of the northwest. Here a furrow can be made with a plow 1,000 miles long, from Winnipeg to the Rocky Mountains—and be but a base line for 1,000 miles square of farming land.

British Columbia, on the Pacific, completes the attractive picture. Here is found not only wide agricultural areas, but also enormous, needed supplies of timber, and sources of fish food unequaled elsewhere in the world. And here are located minerals the extent and value of which far exceed those of all the mineral states on the Pacific Coast—not withstanding the enormous output which, in the last 50 years, they have exhibited.

The half century of opportunity now opening up for the coming American boy and girl must include within its scope this northern region. For it has the best supply of raw material and food products essential to the success of the United States in its attempt to build up a foreign trade.

The possibilities of profit, the field of opportunity, the settlement of numerous questions of international concern, the absorption of immigration, the creation of ready-made customers, and the hope of the future—all these issues rest in a trade that shall be as continental in extent as it is continental in profit.

John Philip
Newman

Methodism And Its Brothers, In One Family

At the time he wrote of the future of Methodism, John Philip Newman (1826-1899) was serving as elected bishop of the Methodist Episcopal Church, stationed in Omaha, Nebraska. He had moved from a series of pastorates in Washington, D.C., and New York City, where he filled the largest M.E. churches. Imagination, a noble presence, and a rich and musical voice comprised his natural gifts, although his thought was not considered profound. Newman had developed a strong friendship with President Ulysses S. Grant and was popularly known as "Grant's pastor."

Bishop Newman wrote several religious volumes between 1870 and 1900, but his preaching built his reputation. He exhibited a rather grandiose style (complete with rehearsed gestures and poses), which used a wealth of allusions and illustrations from literature and foreign travel. This style delighted the prevailing taste, and it promoted his reputation as the leader of an important American sect.

I think that the Methodist Church will awaken in the next century to the importance of doing those things which will enable it to maintain its commanding position among religious denominations. I am inclined to think that one of the most important of the changes which the authorities in the denomination will permit will be the adoption of the Wesley liturgy.

That liturgy, as not many of the present generation know, does not differ in many respects from that of the Church of England or the Protestant Episcopal Church of the United States. It was the liturgy prepared by Charles Wesley for the use of the Methodist Episcopalians in the early days of the denomination. It has been gradually abandoned. There is a strong tendency in the denomination now to return to it, and I have no doubt that early in the next century it will again be adopted.

I shall rejoice if I live to see it. It will put us in closer relations with the great denomination from which we sprang [the Protestant Episcopal Church]. For, the Protestant Episcopal Church, having overthrown those influences which made the organization of the Methodist Church necessary, is now working with mighty zeal for the cause of Christ.

I do not think that the adoption of the Wesley liturgy will cause a return of the Methodists to the Protestant Episcopal Church. The two denominations have peculiarly their own work to do, and in the next century they are going to do it magnificently. They will do it side-by-side, as brothers, after all, in one family.

The religious development of the Twentieth Century is, I think, to keep pace with the magnificent material prosperity which awaits this country. Each will supplement the other.

John
Wanamaker

The Most Businesslike Great Business Machine

The Philadelphia merchant John Wanamaker (1838-1922) served as President Benjamin Harrison's Postmaster General from 1889 to 1893. At the age of 19, he had become the first paid YMCA secretary in the nation. However, Wanamaker soon shifted to dry goods and developed Philadelphia's largest retail clothing business. As a volume retailer, he pioneered the department-store concept, saturation newspaper advertising, and employee-betterment programs. John Wanamaker engaged in extensive philanthropy— most notably involving Presbyterian Sunday-school education and the construction of hospital facilities.

As Harrison's Postmaster General, Wanamaker angered civil-service reformers with his use of the spoils system. Nevertheless, he established several technical improvements in the handling of mail and experimented with rural free delivery. He also advocated parcel-post and postal-savings systems (long before the adoption of either), and he encouraged the federal ownership of the telegraph and telephone services. Wanamaker remained active in his business, religious, and charity endeavors to the end of his long life.

The postal service will be almost entirely electrical 100 years from now. Of course, the railroads, and the steamboats, and the stages, and the horseback riders will still be employed for the carriage of the mails. But all business communications and all communications of all sorts that are really intended to be quick will be transmitted by telegraph and telephone. And both of these means of transmitting intelligence will be very greatly extended generally, as well as applied to all the immediate business of the postal service.

Free delivery will be universal. This and the boxes for the collection, as well as the delivery, of mail at everybody's house and business office will make the postal service more useful. Also, the telephone and the telegraph (with charg-

es reduced so that the people may really use them) will be extended within everyone's reach, and they will make the postal service more useful. And, in the big cities, there will be the use of electrical devices by which the masses of mail in business centers will be whizzed through tubes to receiving stations. All these things will make the postal service so much more useful and so much easier to use that it will be used a hundred times as much one hundred years from now.

Thousands of small offices in the neighborhood of large cities will be abolished because they will be unnecessary. Stations will be established in their stead and, with the free delivery in the villages and out along the lonely star routes, the country will become more thickly populated. The whole service, by reason of the abolition of useless offices and the addition of modern facilities, will be more economically administered.

The country will be divided into postal districts, and routine matters by the thousand will be attended to much more promptly from near postal centers. The United States postal service will be the greatest business machine and the most businesslike great business machine in the world.

David H. Greer

The Influences Of Christianity Will Be Most Stupendous

Born in West Virginia, David Hummell Greer (1844-1919) graduated from Washington College, worked in his father's wholesale house, and read law before entering the Episcopal theological school at Gambier, Ohio (1864). Thereafter he filled a series of ministerial posts in West Virginia, Kentucky, Virginia, and Rhode Island. In 1888 Greer accepted an appointment to St. Bartholomew's in New York City. His preaching, deeply religious but eminently practical, drew large congregations—including such wealthy families as the Vanderbilts.

Greer proved extremely flexible in his churchmanship and ever alert to the problems increasingly created by modern science. His theological volumes show that he was both liberal and compassionate. Some of his most effective socio-religious work was accomplished on New York's East Side, with the homeless and destitute. David Greer became Bishop of New York in 1908. To his Episcopal congregations and his religious projects, Greer devoted his entire adult life.

I am satisfied that we are to have a solution to the mighty problem of temperance. This will come neither in legislative enactments nor in criminal procedure. Rather, I think that temperance is to be gained solely by the influence of the Christian religion.

I used to favor prohibition. But I now think that it will be demonstrated very soon that this does not offer the key to the problem. I also was in favor of stringent criminal legislation, but I have abandoned that idea too. My experience teaches me that, in the future, it will be recognized that the only way permanently to reclaim the victims of intemperance and to prevent others from becoming victims is by the influence which Christian ministers and Christian men and women are to exert.

There is going to be very soon a change in the views with which the Bible is looked upon by great masses of men and women. This change will come to us in the next century, and the results will be stupendous for good. Men and women will no longer read the Bible mechanically. They will not set themselves a stint of so many chapters a day and, having read them, regard themselves as having performed a Christian duty. They will not look upon the Bible as a sort of fetich [sic].

On the contrary, it will be understood that it is a book to be studied. As [John] Ruskin said, it must be dug into that its truths may be brought out. It will no longer be esteemed as gold coin, but as ore, from which glorious and golden truths are to be extracted. When people begin to realize this, they will understand what is meant by the inspiration of this book. It is an inspiration not in the technical sense, but in its influences. There will be new and splendid lights kindled by this modern treatment of the word of God.

Simplicity will take the place of subtlety and vagueness. It will be understood that the lesson of the Old Testament as revealed by this method of reading the Bible is simply this: God is one; God is a Spirit; God is religious. And the lesson of the New Testament, as suggested by Christ's life, is that religion is love. When in the next century this is understood of all men, I have no doubt that the influences of Christianity will be the most stupendous since those exerted in the early days of the church.

There is going to be, too, a change in the methods of public and private benevolence. Free and indiscriminate charity will be almost unknown. It is beginning to be understood that the highest charity is that which guides rather than supports.

Men and women will be taught to help themselves. The aid will be given in an almost concealed manner. Self-respect will be cultivated and self-reliance as well. The greater benevolences will be conducted upon sound business principles. And I presume that, in the next century, those who then live will see something like a solution of these great and hitherto troublesome social and economic problems.

Richard
Mansfield

One Of The Proudest Achievements Of The American Civilization

At the end of the Nineteenth Century, one of the most vivid actors in the American theater was Richard Mansfield (1854-1907). At a time when drama critics decried the strong influence of European theater on the American stage, Mansfield pursued his own nativistic agenda of producing, managing, and acting.

Richard Mansfield was born to an English couple steeped in the arts—particularly opera. After the death of his father, his mother relocated in Boston, and Richard embarked on a painting career. Soon (1877) he switched to the stage, however, and began to appear in both classical and melodramatic roles. Whenever Mansfield could accumulate some capital, he formed his own dramatic company and toured the East and the Midwest. The young man shone as a road director of "large" productions.

As an actor, Mansfield's most memorable roles included Richard III, Shylock, Cyrano de Bergerac, Brutus in Julius Caesar, Ivan the Terrible, and a hallmark Dr. Jekyll and Mr. Hyde. He became the epitome of the romantic tradition in the American theater— both in "grand style" plays and in traditional repertoire. Although a traditional actor, Mansfield proved a daring producer, offering some of the first performances of George Bernard Shaw and Henrik Ibsen in the United States. His perspective on the American stage remained deep inside the art throughout his life.

I presume that the wealthy men of the greater cities will, before many years, give to the drama the same encouragement and liberal support which they have been disposed in this century to bestow upon the other arts. For the perfection of the American drama, we must look very largely to the support of those who have wealth with which to encourage all those influences which tend to greater cultivation of the people.

I presume that, in New York City for instance, we shall have a great theater—perhaps modeled after that of the great theater of France. It will be supported not by the patronage of the state, but by that of individuals of wealth. With such support, the theater in the United States can become the great refining and moral influence which, in its highest form, it has been in France. It will develop actors who are true artists—and whose artistic achievements will be recognized precisely as are the achievements of those who do the best things in other forms of artistic endeavor.

The prizes which await those who successfully portray human nature and life as they are, or as they have existed, will be not only pecuniary ones. They will include also that recognition which society now gives to the great painter or the great writer.

Under the influence of such a theater as I believe will be established, the best stimulus for dramatic workmanship will inspire those who undertake to write plays. We shall therefore have developed not only great artists upon the stage, but great constructors and writers of plays for them. When this condition is reached, the American drama—both in its acting and in its making—will be one of the proudest achievements of the American civilization of the Twentieth Century.

Joseph
Howard, Jr.

The Essence And The Externalities Of Journalism

From the time of his graduation from Rensselaer Polytechnic Institute (Troy, New York) in 1857, Joseph Howard, Jr. (1833-1908) immersed himself in the profession of journalism. For decades he wrote columns over the signature "Howard," and was syndicated from coast to coast and in European papers. Howard proved most prolific—for example, writing in 1863 for the New York Times, *the* Brooklyn Eagle, *the* New York Sunday Mercury, *and such periodicals as the* Atlantic Monthly, The Leader, *and* Noah's Sunday Times.

During the 1870s and 1880s, Howard regularly covered feature events for the New York Star *and the* New York Herald. *He specialized in controversial trials, political campaigns, the deaths of major political figures, and such socio-cultural events as the opening of the Brooklyn Bridge (1883) and the World's Columbian Exposition in Chicago (1893).*

After 1880 Howard wrote independently, selling his columns and features to a wide range of publications. He also lectured regularly on the topic of journalism. Howard's contributions to the profession were recognized in 1895, when he was elected president of the New York Press Club. This dynamic journalist wrote copiously, to the day of his death.

In response to an interviewer, President [Grover] Cleveland once said: "Oh, you saw that in such-and-such a newspaper. You might have known it wasn't true."

On the same day, Thomas Byrnes, superintendent of police in New York City, replying to a question, said: "You might have known that wasn't true. You saw it in the newspapers. Whenever you see anything published there about me or my affairs, you may take it for granted that it is untrue."

As a practical newspaper writer, I naturally regard with the most intense interest every phase of journalism, good and bad. Contemplating possible changes in this greatest of professions made between now and 1993, I naturally examine the data at hand, in order that I may intelligently attempt a forecast.

Some little time since, an esteemed co-worker in the realm of art, William J. LeMoyne, sent me two tiny volumes written by Samuel Patterson in 1753, and published for him by Joseph Johnson in 1772. They are called *Joineriana, or the Book of Scraps*—a series of interesting essays on diverse topics, one of which is entitled "News and News Writers."

If Brother Patterson's photograph of the newspapers 100 years ago is at all accurate, the one and only change in the line of improvement which distinguishes the newspaper press of 1892 from those of a century earlier is in the advanced mechanical facilities at the service of publishers. They then worked the humble and awkward hand press.

Today we have mechanisms marvelous in their ingenious complication and simple withal. The ordinary mind stands confused by the output and embarrassed in its vain endeavor to comprehend the why and the wherefore. It must be remembered that of every 100,000 readers, at least 99,000 never saw a modern printing press at work.

The grandeur of a pressroom is beyond compare. All is quiet. The electric light brightens the subterranean vaults, as though the midday sun in all its glory was effulgent there. Huge rolls of paper, miles in extent, are fastened in their place. The stereotyped plates wait patiently to begin their work of devouring, digesting, and springing forth for the healing of the nations.

With the word, the machinery starts. With the rapidity of the lightning's flight, the wheels merrily turn. And within the hour that roll of paper, miles in length, has poured into the funnel and over the cylinder. It rests now, a mighty pile of 8-, 10-, 20-, 40-paged papers—neatly, accurately printed on both sides, folded with mathematical precision, pasted, and ready for delivery.

The sight is almost uncanny. And it has seemed to me at times, when looking over the rail, I could almost hear these mighty monsters whispering to each other— for they do everything but read.

All this is new.

But a brief reference to the pages of *Joineriana* convinces me that nothing else is changed. "Students," says the writer, "of every class may now burn their books, like so much useless lumber. They can circumscribe their studies hereafter to the newspaper productions of the press." Even the names of today were anticipated: *Gazette; Journal; Ledger; Mercury; Courant; Chronicle;* etc.

According to the writer, 50 years or 70 years before his time "news writers or sober journalists were mere abstractors and brief chroniclers of the time." But, when this was written, the author says, "We commonly discover the writer a curious impertinent, watching the heels of the great, more intent upon their motions than their measures, giving the earliest notice when his lordship stole out of town, and also when her ladyship was happily delivered to the great joy of that noble family."

Obviously newspapers of the then and newspapers of the now are as like as two peas in a single pod.

"Newspapers," continues our author, "as they have been carried on of late years are a standing reproach to the nation. Every species of guilt, every mode of extravagance, every method of gambling, and every possible way of subverting order and setting the laws at defiance are daily intimated, comforted, and propagated by our news writers."

Just so here.

Within the past 10 years, there has grown a habit in some of our most influential journals of private prosecution which has developed into individual persecution of the most inhuman type. We have officers of the law whose duty it is to detect crime, arrest, try, and punish criminals. Nevertheless, certain newspapers, instigated thereto by hope of gain, have taken it upon themselves to ferret out every particle of evidence and to make it impossible for an accused man to have a fair chance in a modern court of justice. Judges are brow-beaten, lawyers are intimidated, and jurors find their footsteps dogged by spacework scribblers. All of these officers of the court find the literal sanctity of their own domesticity intruded upon and spied upon by sneak reporters.

Was it so then?

Read and ponder. Says the author: "Errors in conduct were condemned formerly as now, but the delinquent was not left hopeless. His future virtues might repair his past indiscretions. At present the error, magnified and tortured by misrepresentation, is irreparable. He is held up in scorn and derision. Those that go by shake their heads and make mouths at him.

"A paper without murders and robberies and rapes and incest and bestiality and sodomy and sacrilege and incendiary letters and forgeries and executions and duels and suicides is said to be void of news. Newspapers are no longer what they were originally intended to be—chronicles of events—but firebrands which it behooves every honest man to quench."

And so on and on and on. In other words, I find absolutely no data outside of the composing room, the stereotype room, and the pressroom on which to formulate any forecast whatever.

It is a somewhat remarkable fact that human nature has never changed. The first family, so far as recorded history shows, exhibited in the Garden of Eden every passion known to the present race—love, hate, jealousy, cruelty, murder, envy, curiosity, disobedience. All of these characterized the ongoing of Adam and Eve, Cain, Abel, and the rest.

We wear a different style of garment externally, but the heart remains the same. Journalism in its earlier period, in its Edenic state, was precisely as it is today, so far as material goes and so far as it sought to influence mankind. It differs only in its externalities, its paper, its type, its presswork, and the machinery by which this magnificent transformation has been effected.

This is the age of electricity.

It is not too much to predict that, ere another decade has past, electricity will be the prime motor directing the great mechanisms of the world. Twenty years ago a four-cylinder press was a marvel. Look at the wonderful instruments at the beck and call of capital today.

In just the last quarter of a century, these marvelous improvements have been effected. And they are so wonderful as to afford no possible basis of contrast or comparison with the facilities at the hand of our brothers of 100 years ago. So, in this restless time—when years are crowded into months and months into days, when every nerve is strained and every muscle swells that the wild rush for wealth and power may be maintained—it is not unreasonable to predict still greater changes in the physical complements of a well-furnished daily newspaper establishment.

But the rest?

Ah, the rest remains with him who, for his own wise purpose, started and has carried along with infinite mercy and wonderful forbearance this extraordinary race of mankind. So long as men are built as they are today—mentally, morally, and physically—human nature cannot change. And until human nature changes the outwork, the output cannot be expected to alter. Would you expect to pluck figs from thistles or to find the juicy grape on the bending boughs of a royal oak? Our mental equipments are as they are—steered in every human individual by passions divinely implanted and divinely permitted, if not divinely encouraged.

Changes in journalism?

I fail to see the sign.

How is it with thee, my brother?

Rafael
Joseffy

The Greatest Music-Producing Nation On Earth

Born in Hungary, Rafael Joseffy (1852-1915) possessed inherent talent that brought him thorough training in the piano, beginning in Budapest at the age of eight. At 14 he entered the Leipzig Conservatorium and then moved (1868) to Berlin to work under Tausig. To this mentor accrues the credit for Joseffy's musical ideas and brilliant concert technique.

Throughout the 1870s, Rafael Joseffy toured Europe to unbounded acclaim for his quality of tone, clean-cut phrasing, and stage presence. In 1879 he arrived in the United States and, for two years, stunned concert audiences with his brilliant technique. Critics heralded Joseffy as the heir to Franz Liszt.

Then, at the height of his fame, Joseffy withdrew from the public stage and spent five years studying intensively to discover the deeper levels of his art. He returned (1886) to the concert platform a more mature, more sensitive interpreter of the classical composers. Joseffy excelled as a player of Bach and Mozart, but also mastered presenting the works of Beethoven, Schumann, Chopin, Liszt, and Brahms.

In the 1890s, at the peak of his American renown, Joseffy withdrew entirely from public performances and devoted himself to writing, to editing, and to teaching at the National Conservatory in New York City. He published two volumes of his own views on piano technique and interpretation (1902; 1913), and he edited collections of Liszt, Brahms, and particularly Chopin (1915). Although Joseffy's work as a composer was inconsequential, his influence as a master of technique and a teacher was significant.

I do not believe that, in the next century, any greater pianists will be heard than some of those who have lived in the Nineteenth Century. It would be impossible to master that noble instrument to any greater extent than some of the men who have gained immortality by such achievement have done. The Nineteenth Century has been the era of the triumph of the piano.

But it is wholly possible that there may come mechanical improvements which will make it possible to exceed the victories of some of the great pianists of this era. Everybody knows that, if it were possible to secure a greater division of the scale than is now obtained upon pianos, there might be some astonishing and delightful triumphs. But such a discovery would revolutionize music.

The mechanical improvements in the piano have already been wonderful. Every pianist, how-ever, has at times realized some of the still un-conquerable mechanical difficulties of the in-strument. And perhaps the greater triumphs of the greater pianists have been the overcoming of these difficulties.

The future of music in the United States is assured. It is going to be a great music-loving nation, as it even is today, but it is to be an appre-ciative and understanding love. I shall not be at all surprised if, in the next century, the United States stands in the same relation to music which Germany has had for the past 200 years. There will be great composers, great artists, and great singers who will receive most generous support from the people.

Even in my own experience, the strides of musical development have been prodigious in this country. If they keep on, it will be a nation in which exquis-ite melody and glorious harmony will express the artistic truth that is in music to a people capable of comprehending it. Yes, I think that the United States in the next century will be the greatest music-loving and music-producing nation on earth.

Abram
Dittenhoefer

The All-Around
Lawyer Will Be
A Rara Avis

*The family of Abram Jesse Dittenhoefer (1836-1919) moved from South Caro-
lina to New York City when he was four years old. After attending Columbia College (1855), Abram read law with a New York firm and was admitted to the bar in
1857. He then fashioned a legal career that meshed the representation of major financial
institutions, corporations, and insurance companies with specialties in copyright and
theatrical law. For example, he handled the incorporation of the Actors Fund of America
(1882) and served for years as its counsel without compensation.*

*A strong Lincoln Republican, Dittenhoefer led the German Republican Central
Committee of New York for 12 years and appeared as a delegate at numerous national
Republican conventions. Despite his influential political ties, Dittenhoefer eschewed
elective office himself. He preferred and excelled with intricate theatrical problems of
creative rights and performance.*

In my opinion, there are to be witnessed in the next century some very striking
changes in the relation of the legal profession to its clients—and, to some extent, in the practice of law.

Since I have been at the bar, I have noticed the growth of the tendency to
divide the practice of law into specialties. It is not so very long ago that every
lawyer accepted all sorts of practice. There, of course, always have been lawyers
who have been known and identified as criminal lawyers, as distinguished from
practitioners who have confined their practice to the civil branches of the law.

I do not refer, however, to that kind of specialty practice. What I mean is
that I think, early in the next century, it will be found that pretty generally through-

out the United States lawyers will—by special study in one or another of the branches of civil law—attract to their offices only that sort of practice involved in the branch of which they have made a study. They will become specialists. This is now true to some extent of lawyers in New York City and some of the other great cities of the land.

Now this segregation, so to speak, is bound to continue more and more. By the next century, I suspect that what we now know as an all-around lawyer will be a very rara avis.

There is another thing which is going to have an enormous influence in changing the methods of the bar of this country. The facility of communication between the rural sections and the larger cities is probably going to be greatly increased. Thus, in the next century, almost every community or town will be within speaking distance of the greater cities.

Distances will be obliterated. I suspect that, as a result, the old-fashioned country lawyer—the man who has done everything from drawing a deed and a will to defending a criminal in the local courts—will become very largely a tradition. This facility of communication will take those who have legal business to the cities. For that reason, I expect to see the number of lawyers in the cities be proportionately greater than is now the case, while the number of country lawyers will be proportionately less. There will in fact be no country lawyers.

I do not think that the rewards which the ablest practitioners in the next century will gain will be any larger than have been some of those earned in the past 30 years. As the number of specialists (and able specialists, too) in the practice of law increases, the business now obtained by the few great specialists will be considerably divided up. There will be more able specialists—a great many more than there are today.

For that reason, there will not be so many examples of prodigious individual earnings. However, I suspect that the lads of today—who will be ready to practice law throughout the first half of the next century—will average more earnings than those lads who began the practice of law 30 years ago.

Further, I am inclined to think that the achievements of the bar of the Twentieth Century will probably exceed in brilliancy, on the whole, those of the bar of the Nineteenth Century. There are some great questions coming up which we now only vaguely perceive. These will be determined very largely through the influence of the bar—just as the Constitutional questions of the present century have been settled by the American bar.

George F. Kunz

The Production And Use Of Precious Stones

At a very early age, George Frederick Kunz (1856-1935) demonstrated a remarkable gift for geological research and an appreciation of precious stones. Born in New York City and schooled at Cooper Union, he became a gem expert at the age of 23 with Tiffany and Company (1879). From 1883 to 1909, Kunz served as a special agent of the U.S. Geological Survey. In this capacity he represented the United States at a series of international expositions (1889-1904), usually organizing the precious-stones exhibits.

Kunz became a vice president at Tiffany and Company in 1907, a position he held until his death. He gained worldwide fame as an explorer for gems, and he was a recognized authority on ancient jewelry. Kunz also served as the research curator of precious stones for the American Museum of Natural History.

His interests ranged widely, however—from membership in the North American Indian Memorial Commission, to the presidency of the American Metric Association, to a leadership role in campaigns to save and extend New York City's parks system. The author of several volumes on gems and precious stones, George Kunz also wrote numerous magazine articles and pamphlets on gems, minerals, folklore, and antiquities.

I am inclined to think that the opal mines of the State of Washington and the turquoise mines in New Mexico are going to produce gems equal to the opals found in the Ural Mountains and to the turquoise of Persia, respectively. Already they have taken from the New Mexican mines a turquoise which is as fine as anything that Persian mines have yielded. And some of the opals from Washington are certainly very beautiful gems.

I also think that, in the near future, we are going to see a wonderful development in the use of jewels in American churches. The tendency has already been set in that direction. In one of the churches of the West, there are jewels used by the priest in his offices worth many thousands of dollars. The Bishop of Long Island and the Bishop of Springfield have received costly jewels that they wear in performing their offices. And in two of the churches in New York City there are adornments of precious stones which represent a great deal of money.

My impression is that, in the next century, it will be found that—in many of the churches of the United States—jewels of rare beauty and great cost will serve the priests for the greater adornment of their chancels and their vestments. We shall, I think, equal if not exceed the use of jewels as an accessory for the priestly offices which has characterized some of the churches of the European continent. Precious stones—even beautiful marbles—will more and more be utilized for impressive religious ceremony.

Daniel W. Voorhees

Only Minor Changes In Our System Of Government

Although educated as an attorney, Daniel Wolsey Voorhees (1827-1897) spent most of his life as a politician. Born in Ohio and raised in Indiana, Daniel graduated from Indiana Asbury (De Pauw) University in 1849. He read law and was admitted to the Indiana bar two years later. After an unsuccessful campaign for the U.S. Congress in 1856, the young man moved his practice to Terre Haute.

From 1858 to 1861, Voorhees served as the U.S. District Attorney for Indiana. He then was elected to the U.S. House of Representatives (1861-1866; 1869-1873) and subsequently to the Senate (1877-1897). As a staunch Democrat, he built a reputation as a champion of agrarian interests and of a large, freely-circulating currency.

The Senator was tall and heavy, with fair hair and dark eyes. He acquired the sobriquet of the "Tall Sycamore of the Wabash" and was unrivalled in the Midwest as a stump speaker and forensic orator. Personally he was generous to a fault. As a result, Voorhees died poor, despite a lucrative law practice in Indiana.

In my judgment the next 100 years will show but slight changes in the form of our government. A century hence, I should expect to see (were I upon earth) the American republic governed very much as it is at the present day.

Some minor changes, however, are altogether probable. Among these I should think would likely be a limit of the Presidential term to six years, with no re-election, and a change in the manner of choosing the President and Vice-President. But these are subsidiary alterations merely; they will not affect the structure of the government.

I take it that the American people decided at the recent [1892] election against any further centralization of power in this country. For instance, I believe they have decided that there shall be no federal control of elections within the states. This decision—if I am right in assuming that the election means that—has greater significance than most people attach to it.

The significance is that the limits of our federal powers are now pretty well-defined, and that the people do not wish them to be either circumscribed or greatly enlarged. For this reason, I believe the government will go through another century substantially as it is at the present day. We apparently have reached that golden mean between two possible extremes. To me the lesson of the election is that the people will jealously watch every effort made to shift the balance in one direction or the other.

One hundred years hence, this country will probably have a system of customs taxation that will approximate free trade as closely as anything which the world now knows. I believe we shall always have custom houses and that there will always be tariffs for them to collect. But a century hence, I should be very much surprised to return to earth and find such a system of taxation as we now have. We shall approach our ultimate approximation of free trade very slowly, and cautiously, and in such manner as to cause no violent injustice to any interest.

Within the life of the man now grown, the changes may be considerable, but they will not be revolutionary. Within the present generation, I look to see a considerable part of the money needed for our government raised by means of an income tax. I believe the day is fast approaching in which our people will insist upon taxing the property and the prosperity of the country—not its necessities.

Alfred
Van Santvoord

An Enormous System Of Inland Merchant Marine

Perhaps no one in the United States in 1892 was better qualified to discuss the topic of water freighting than Commodore Alfred Van Santvoord (1819-1901). His father, Abram Van Santvoord (1784-1858), had pioneered Hudson River steamboat and barge transportation early in the Nineteenth Century with steamboat-developer Robert Fulton.

Alfred was born in Utica, New York, and educated in common schools. At an early age he joined his father's business, and the two men built a successful freighting trade on the Erie Canal. "Commodore" Van Santvoord then expanded the family business into passenger and steamboat transport in the New York City area. During the Civil War, he chartered a number of boats to the federal government, at considerable remuneration.

Thereafter Van Santvoord built a shipping empire by integrating steamboat travel, railroad freighting, and barge hauling—relying heavily on canals to establish his network. In 1890 he became the president and principal owner of the Hudson River Day Line of steamboats, which ran between New York City and Albany. A member of numerous New York City clubs, Alfred also served as a director of the Chicago, Milwaukee and St. Paul Railway, the Delaware and Hudson Railroad, and the United Railways of New Jersey. He was an enthusiastic yachtsman and owned the exceptional steam yacht Clermont, on which he died in 1901.

I do not believe that Robert Fulton's invention of the paddle wheel will ever be improved on for inland navigation. There may be some improvements in minor details, but the principle of the paddle wheel will remain supreme.

I am inclined to think, however, that it may be possible in the next century to go from New York to Chicago or to Duluth—and possibly from New York to New Orleans—on inland waterways by steamboat. If a ship canal is cut across New York State (and it is entirely within the bounds of probability that this will be done early in the next century), and another is cut from Chicago to the Mississippi River, then it will be possible to make this trip by steamboat. The probabilities are, however, that navigation of this sort will be made by screw propellers for the most part, rather than by the side-wheel boat.

I think the development of an inland marine is going to be something prodigious in the next century. While railroad construction was going on as rapidly as has been the case in the last 30 years, inland marine development was checked. It is now again attracting the attention of the great capitalists. The tonnage through the ship canal at Sault Ste. Marie has been the greatest in the world, and that canal has been enlarged only within recent years.

We shall find the solution to some of the railway problems in the development of this inland marine. And, if the greater canals are dug (which capitalists even now are considering) in the Twentieth Century, people then alive will see an enormous system of inland merchant marine. This development will be every bit as extensive as are the railway systems which control the great trunk lines.

John J.
Ingalls

Remarkable Changes In Everyday Life

Born in Middleton, Massachusetts, John James Ingalls (1833-1900) graduated from Williams College in 1855. He then studied law for two years, prior to being admitted to the Massachusetts bar. But Ingalls was drawn west, and he located in the boom town of Sumner, Kansas, in 1858. Two years later he moved to Atchison and became deeply involved in Civil War politics. Ingalls served as secretary of the Kansas Territorial Council (1860), secretary of the first state senate (1861), and state senator (1862). Simultaneously he served as judge advocate in the Kansas militia.

Ingalls remained with the Republican Party and was rewarded with a seat in the U.S. Senate (1873-1891). During his last term, he was president pro tempore of the Senate.

Ingalls built a national reputation as an orator—one particularly adept in denunciation. An admirer stated: "Standing cold and motionless, John Ingalls could pour out a flood of vitriolic abuse and blasting party misrepresentation suggestive of John Randolph."

After his defeat at the hands of the Populists in 1890, Ingalls devoted his time to lecturing and writing. His oratorical skills made him a popular lyceum performer, especially in the Midwest and the West. Although he remained a practicing attorney, Senator Ingalls proved a greater financial success as a speaker and observer of American life.

Man, having conquered the earth and the sea, will complete his dominion over nature by the subjugation of the atmosphere. This will be the crowning triumph of the coming century.

Long before 1993, the journey from New York City to San Francisco, across the continent, and from New York City to London, across the sea, will be made between the sunrise and sunset of a summer day. The railway and the steamship will be as obsolete as the stagecoach. And it will be as common for the citizen to call for his dirigible balloon as it now is for his buggy or his boots. Electricity will be the motive power, and aluminium or some lighter metal will be the material of the aerial cars, which will navigate the abyss of the sky.

The electric telegraph will be supplanted by the telephone, which will be perfected and simplified. Telephone instruments, located in every house and office, will permit the communication of business and society to be conducted by the voice at will from Boston to Moscow and Hoang-Ho, just as readily as now between neighboring villages.

This will dispose of the agitation of the proposition to take the railroads and telegraphs away from those who own them and give them to those who do not.

Domestic life and avocations will be rendered easier, less costly, and less complex by the distribution of light, heat, and energy through storage cells or from central electric stations. Thus the "servant problem" will cease to disturb. Woman, having more leisure, will elevate her political and social status from subordination to equality with man.

The contest between brains and numbers, which began with the birth of the race, will continue to its extinction. The struggle will be fierce and more relentless in the coming century than ever before in the history of humanity. But brains will keep on top, as usual. As before, those who fail will outnumber those who succeed.

Wealth will accumulate, business will combine, and the gulf between the rich and the poor will be more profound. But wider education and greater activity of the moral forces of the race ultimately will compel recognition of the fact that the differences between men are organic and fundamental—that they result from an act of God and cannot be changed by an act of Congress.

The attempt to abolish poverty, pay debts, and cure the ills of society by statute will be the favorite prescription of ignorance, incapacity, and credulity for the next 100 years—as it has been from the beginning of civilization.

The condition in the United States is unprecedented, in that all the implacables and malcontents are armed with the ballot. Thus, if they are unanimous, they can control the purse and the sword by legislation. Nevertheless, the

perception exists that the social and political condition here, with all its infir-
mities, remains immeasurably the best. This perception will undoubtedly make
our system permanent and preserve it even against essential modifications.

Our greatest city in 1993? Chicago! It is a vortex, with a constantly increasing
circumference, into which the wealth and population of the richest and most
fertile area of the earth's surface is constantly concentrating. When this anniversary returns, Chicago will be not only the greatest city in the United States,
but also in the world.

Matthew C. D.
Borden

American Cotton Will Control World Markets

Fall River, Massachusetts, not only was the birth place of Matthew Chaloner Durfee Borden (1842-1913), but it also became the location of some of his greatest financial and commercial successes. Borden gained his early education at Phillips Academy (Andover), and he graduated from Yale College in 1864. He moved immediately into the New York City business world, developing interests in dry-goods firms, brokerages, and printing corporations.

In 1889 Borden erected three immense cloth mills in Fall River. These facilities spun yarn and wove the same into cloth for printing; he added a fourth mill in 1895. Borden's residence remained in New York City, however, where he served as a director of the Manhattan Bank, the Lincoln Bank, the Lincoln Safe Deposit Company, and the New York Security and Trust Company. He also held memberships in scores of the city's most prestigious clubs. With authority, Matthew Borden could speak of the future of the cotton industry.

Cotton manufacturing in the South has come to stay. It is going to be greatly developed in the next century and will be of vast benefit to that section of the country. The number of mills will be greatly increased, and the quality of the product will be steadily improved. This will add millions to the wealth of the cotton-producing states.

The pre-eminence of the New England states in cotton manufacturing will not, however, be threatened by this great and healthy development in the South. I do not look for any serious competition between the manufacturers of the two sections.

Yet I am inclined to think that, in the next century, it will be found that American cotton manufacturers will have wrested the markets of the world from the great manufacturers of England, who have for the greater part of this century controlled these markets. Just as surely as the tide rises, just so surely American cotton goods in the next century are going to command the markets of the world. We have already almost reached that point. We are competing in some sections of the world with Manchester, and successfully.

I think this is true, too, of many other lines of American manufactures. Our people are slowly, perhaps, but surely reaching the time when American goods will be in greater demand than those produced in Great Britain or upon the continent of Europe. In the next century, the dawn of that day when our manufacturing supremacy is acknowledged will be witnessed—and, I think, by many people who are now living.

The commercial development of the United States in the Twentieth Century will be prodigious. Those of us who are in business life get some hint of it now. It is clear to me that, while we are to be the greatest agricultural nation in the world, we are also just as surely reaching forward for commercial and manufacturing supremacy. It is going to be a great century to live in, this one which begins seven years hence.

Joaquin Miller

Man Is Not A Bad Animal At All

The decision of Cincinnatus Hiner Miller (1839-1913) to adopt the colorful first name of "Joaquin" is indicative of this poet's iconoclastic approach to life.

He was born in Indiana, the son of a Quaker schoolmaster. "Nat's" family lived in Illinois before settling in the new Oregon country in 1852. The boy left home at 17 to try the California gold camps. He then spent a year living with a band of Digger Indians before returning to Oregon to teach school, read law, and gain admittance to the Oregon bar (1861).

Miller edited the (Eugene, Oregon) Democratic Register in 1863, and then he focused on the writing of poetry with a Western flare. Following only minor local response, the poet retreated to England (1871), where his reception as a frontier-American artist was overwhelming. Through the 1870s and 1880s, Miller published myriad volumes of poetry, drama, and prose, none of it of exceptional merit. In the late 1880s, the eccentric, bearded sage settled permanently in Oakland, California—from where he pontificated on every aspect of American society and culture. The man was not without opinions!

I am not wise or learned in things-to-be, but I will venture a few predictions. In the first place, our government will be less complex and go forward year after year with less friction and better results—like an improved machine. We will cut off the foreign vote, the ignorant vote, and the verdant vote.

As we grow better in body and mind, venerable men will have their place of honor, as of old. If a good man by temperance, healthful toil, and wise care preserves his body and mind—like [William] Gladstone, for example—he has saved the life of at least one citizen, a brave thing to do of old.

And it is not fit that such a man should be put in a prize ring to fight with lusty young adventurers for his place in the senate. It is already his by right. Let

10,000 entirely qualified voters, representing at least 100,000,000 people, send up to the state capital their oldest man, and it is all on the register. Let the state then send to Washington its two oldest Gladstones as senators—and so on up to the President, and so on down to the justice of the peace. What a saving of time, temper, manhood, money! When we have grown a generation or two of

[Allen G.] Thurmans, [James G.] Blaines, and Gladstones, we will leave elections in the hands of God, where we found them. This is my plan, my prophecy.

As for cities, we will build new ones, on pleasant, beautiful sites, as men now build hotels. Even now millions are waiting for those who will build a new city—complete with sewers, pipes, pavements, all things—and empty the unclean and rotten old into the healthful and pleasant new. We are going to have great cities, such as have not been. Whereabouts I do not know, but all the world is going to town. Machinery has emancipated man from the fields.

What about big fortunes? Well, I think we will some day require the bulk of the rich man's money (when he is done with it, of course) to build national parks with—and in other ways to help the nation which helped him to get hold of it.

As for literature, our writers will surely soon turn back to the oriental or the ideal—as against the realistic school—and remain there. They cannot very well improve on the Bible, Arabian tales, or Shakespeare. Meanwhile the sensational and personal newspapers of today will disappear down the sluice and sewer of indictable nuisances.

Discoveries? Truly it seems to me that very soon some new [Christopher] Columbus will come from among us to launch his airships on the great high seas and gulf streams that surge and roll above us. Yet maybe this faith is founded on what has been, rather than on any sign of what is to be.

Who will be best remembered? Why, [Thomas] Edison, of course.

Yes, most certainly we will be handsomer, healthier, happier too, and ergo better—for man is not a bad animal at all, if he only has half a chance to be good. And he certainly has such a chance to be good now, and to do good, too, as never was known before. And he will do his best with it. Let us believe in him and trust him entirely, for in that way is the good God.

Warner Miller

The Nicaraguan Canal Is Inevitable

This committed advocate of the Nicaraguan canal project was born to German parents at Hannibal, New York. Warner Miller (1838-1918) was educated locally and then graduated from Union College at Schenectady (1860). He embarked on a career teaching Greek and Latin at Fort Edward Collegiate Institute, but the Civil War interrupted, and Miller joined the New York Volunteer Cavalry.

After the war, the young man purchased a paper mill in Herkimer and developed new processes to produce paper from wood pulp. By the late 1870s, he had earned a reputation as a leader in the industry and served as president of the American Paper and Pulp Association. Miller's corporate success drew him into the arena of politics.

An active and influential Republican, Miller was elected to the New York State Assembly (1873-1876), to the U.S. House of Representatives (1879-1881), and to the U.S. Senate (1881-1887). Throughout his public service, the politician carried strong nationalistic attitudes, favored the development of a dominant merchant marine, and endorsed the protective tariff.

Warner Miller became a knowledgeable advocate of the Nicaraguan canal project and one of the proposal's most adamant boosters. In 1903 Congress selected the isthmian route through Panama rather than that through Nicaragua; the Panama Canal began to handle interocean traffic in 1914.

In the early years of the next century, it is going to be possible to go by steamer from New York to San Francisco, or the South American countries, without making the trip through the Straits of Magellan. The Nicaraguan canal is as sure to be built as tides are to ebb and flow and the seasons to change. If the United States does not build it—either by private subscription or through the encouragement of the government—it will be built by those who live in other lands. The canal is inevitable, and the effect of its construction upon the destiny of the United States is something almost inconceivable.

It is to be as conspicuous an engineering triumph of the next century as the Suez Canal was of this. The tonnage which will be carried through it will, within five years after opening, exceed the tonnage that passes through Suez. No man can accurately forecast its effect upon the railway problems of the United States, but it will be enormous. It is going to furnish means for the development of the magnificent wealth of the South American countries and—if the United States controls the canal, or United States capital does—this development will be enormously to our own advantage.

I cannot speak with enough enthusiasm of this vast undertaking, which is to see its triumph in the Twentieth Century. I do not believe any man, however vivid his imagination, can fully suggest the enormous influence which this artificial water highway will have upon the commercial destiny of the United States. If I should suggest one-half of what I believe to be possible, I might be regarded as an absurd dreamer.

Sidney G.
Brock

Perfect Government, Improved People

At the time Sidney Gorham Brock (1837-1918) penned his predictions on American society, he was serving as Chief of the Bureau of Statistics in the Treasury Department in Washington, D.C. This man of diverse interests was particularly well-fitted for the position.

Born in Cleveland, Ohio, Brock received a degree with honors from Allegheny College in Pennsylvania (1859). After distinguished service in the Civil War, he located in Macon, Missouri, where he practiced law and published the Macon Republican. *Brock served three terms as mayor of Macon (1886-1888) and then ran an unsuccessful campaign for the U.S. House of Representatives (1888). This hard-fought election brought Brock to the attention of President Benjamin Harrison who appointed him (1889) to the Treasury position.*

Brock spent his post-political years writing books on topics of diplomatic interest, including Alaska, Hawaii, navigation in the Great Lakes, and trade across the Pacific Rim. In 1892 he published his most popular work, The Advance of the United States for a Hundred Years, from 1790 to 1890—*so he was peculiarly well-qualified to peer into the future of American life.*

I believe that, in 1993, we in the United States will have the most perfect republican form of government that was ever conceived in the minds of the wisest statesmen. By then the social condition of the people will be such that there will be no suffering from the deprivation of the necessities of life.

All will have happy homes. Vice and immorality will have largely, if not altogether, ceased to exist. There will be not only great intellectual advancement, but also very great moral advancement. We are making wonderful strides in that direction now. There will be less government than there is now, and it will be more simple.

There is no likelihood that the railroads and telegraphs will ever be managed by the state. The state would no more take charge of these industries than it would other enterprises now owned and controlled by individuals—streetcar lines, manufactures, steamship lines, and farms. For, were the state to do such, individual enterprise and opportunities would largely cease. There would be no incentive, or comparatively none, for invention or for individual effort of any kind. All citizens would simply become wards of the nation. They would receive their portions from the state and would return to inaction or indolent effort.

Probably the government will then own and control all the products of our gold and silver mines. These products will be held by the government, as now, for the purpose of redeeming the paper obligations of the government. However, such redemption will largely be unnecessary—for the reason that there will be such stability in our financial laws that the people will not question the value of any of the obligations of the government.

The people by this time will have become educated to such an extent that the vice of intemperance will largely cease. Saloons or public drinking places will probably no longer exist. And stimulants of any kind, if used at all, will probably be only seen in the family.

Improved methods of treatment for the confinement and punishment of criminals will be inaugurated. Much more attention will be given to their reformation than to their punishment.

Wealth undoubtedly will be much more evenly distributed. There will be great comfort and prosperity with the masses as well. The condition of the laboring classes will be less dependent and greatly improved. There will be more friendly relations existing between employers and the employees—better understanding and greater equality.

Methods of agriculture will be such and the improvement in agricultural machinery so great that all the immense population of 1993 will be amply provided for. American citizens will continue to be the best dressed, the best fed, and the best housed people of the world.

There will be great advancement in all the professions in literature, music, and the drama. People will be longer lived. They will understand much better the nature of their wants and the treatment of diseases. They will be better natured and more conciliatory; consequently there will be less need of the laws and laws' methods.

The whole tendency of the race will be toward comfort, leisure, luxury, cultivation, simplicity in dress, and broader charity in all social relations. The race will be handsomer, healthier, and happier than ever before in the history of the world.

John
Habberton

Of Women, Literature, Temperance, Marriage, Etc.

As an editor and author, John Habberton (1842-1921) remained an observer of American society throughout his life. John's father died when the boy was six, and John was shipped from his home town of Brooklyn to Illinois to live with an uncle. In 1859 he returned to New York City and learned the printing trade. After service in the Union Army (1862-1865), Habberton took a position with Harper and Brothers. By 1874 John was literary editor of the Christian Union and then moved to the New York Herald *as its literary and drama critic (1876-1893). He subsequently edited* Godey's Magazine *and wrote for* Collier's Weekly.

In the field of popular fiction, however, Habberton gained his widest acclaim. In 1876 he wrote Helen's Babies, *a work of fiction based on the antics of his adolescent sons. The popular and financial success of this work prompted Habberton to write some three dozen additional pieces of light fiction (1877-1908). All of his works deal with ordinary events in the everyday life of ordinary people. Habberton's only attempt at drama,* Deacon Crankett, *proved a huge success on Broadway and on tour.*

When the people of the United States celebrate the 500th Columbian anniversary, in 1993, there will be so many of them that no longer will it be said that:

> Uncle Sam is rich enough
> To give us all a farm.

Consequently all soil worth tilling will receive the best possible attention—

with the result that we will be the best fed nation in the world. All the forests will be gone. Lumber will be so scarce that stone, iron, brick, slag, etc., will be largely used in the construction of houses. As a result, fires will be almost un-heard of, and insurance companies will go out of business.

The government will be much simpler than now and concern itself with fewer and more im-portant affairs. Indeed, the idea of government will have disappeared. The people will toler-ate nothing more than an administration, on business principles, of such general interests as are too great or complex to be intrusted to private management.

Law will be made for man—not man for the law. Theology will give place to Christian practice, and each man's faith will be judged by his life instead of his talk. Medicine will be practiced at police stations and among outcasts, for respectable people will have resolved that illness not caused by accident is disgracefully criminal. The race will, therefore, be healthier and happier than now, as well as more sensible.

Literature will be much cleaner in the departments of poetry, fiction, and drama. For the already moribund humbug of passion masquerading as love will have died of self-contempt.

Temperance legislation will be not only a dead issue, but so long buried that no one will be able to identify its grave. Proper cooking and improved physi-cal habits will have neutralized the desire for stimulants.

All marriages will be happy—for the law will put to death any man or woman who assumes conjugal position without the proper physical, mental, and financial qualifications. As a natural consequence, the characters for love stories will be selected not from overgrown boys and girls, but from among the men and women longest married.

Women will dress for health instead of for show, trusting their healthy faces to do all the necessary "keeping up appearances."

The servant question will cease to be a burning one, for the rage for display will be outworn. The kitchen stove will give place to ranges heated by water-gas, and men and children as well as women will know how to cook. People of means will eat to live—not live to eat. All household labor will be esteemed too honorable and important to be intrusted to menials.

Woman will have equal rights with man. She will be free to select a hus-band instead of waiting for a man to ask her hand. Nevertheless, in looking backward into literature and tradition, she will wonder whether she has more rights in this respect than her great-great-grandmother enjoyed.

Perhaps I am wrong in some of these prophecies, but if so I shall not be here to be twitted with it—now will I?

Edgar W.
Howe

Society Must Move Toward Simplicity, Honesty, And Truth

Like other successful journalists of the period, Edgar Watson Howe (1853-1937) received much of his education by working as a printer. The Howe family moved from Indiana to northern Missouri in 1856, and Edgar joined (1864) his father in the Fairview newspaper office at the age of 11. He left home to set type in nearby Gallatin in 1868; during the next five years he worked in St. Joseph, Council Bluffs, Omaha, Cheyenne, and Salt Lake City. His attempt to publish a paper in Golden, Colorado, in 1872 proved unsuccessful.

In 1877 Howe and his older brother created the (Atchison, Kansas) Daily Globe. By emphasizing local events and advertisers, this paper became a long-term financial success. For this forum Edgar Howe began writing pithy, pungent editorial paragraphs that frequently were quoted by newspapers from coast to coast. In general, Howe's approach to life was one of "hard work, attention to business, and shrewdness, as well as goodness and fair dealing." One of his dominant themes became simplicity and its necessity in an increasingly complex world.

In 1883 Edgar Howe published the first and most important of his many books, The Story of a Country Town. Depicting the stark life in a frontier homestead community (much like Fairview, Missouri), this work remains a landmark in American literature—the precursor of works of small-town realism like Sherwood Anderson's Winesburg, Ohio (1919) and Sinclair Lewis's Main Street (1920). Upon his death (1937), fellow Kansas journalist William Allen White called Howe "that gentle, kindly old grouch." Edgar Howe had earned the honor.

I think that the growth of America in the next 100 years will be toward simplicity.

The decade just closing has been noted for high pressure, a dissipation of energy. A good many of our customs are worrying, but in reality they do not pay.

During the next century, I believe the American people will learn the important lesson that simple and honest living is the goal to which men should bend their energies. No nation has learned this lesson as it should have been learned. The wonderful Americans will accomplish this result and distinguish themselves more than ever before.

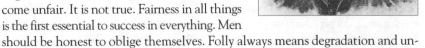

Heretofore we have taught that men should be honest and just for the sake of religion or for the sake of society. The truth is, each individual should be honest and just to benefit himself primarily, and religion and society incidentally.

Many Americans now believe that they might become rich if they would consent to become unfair. It is not true. Fairness in all things is the first essential to success in everything. Men should be honest to oblige themselves. Folly always means degradation and unhappiness.

The old races of men were cruel in the name of patriotism and religion. The men who live in 1993 will be just because their conscience and well-being demand it.

The men of the next century will realize, as the men of no previous century have realized, that simplicity and honesty are the great helps in living. Nonsense has been so respectable in the past that half the people took off their hats to it. But the coming man will discard much of what has worried us and caused us to neglect those simple interests on which our happiness really depended.

Half the things about which we worry are not of the slightest consequence. The coming man will know this, and he will have the greatest regard for the simple truth—about which there need be no doubt. So many men have lived and left histories that no one need go astray.

The truth has always been mixed with nonsense. The men who will celebrate the fifth American centennial will have separated the chaff from the wheat. No teacher of nonsense will be encouraged, even should he claim that his object is to do good. The great truth then will be that, while the necessity for simplicity and honesty has always been taught, it has never been insisted upon as its importance deserved.

The splendid men of the century just dawning will know better than we do that every individual is guaranteed equal rights in life, liberty, and the pursuit of happiness—not by constitutions and governments, but by the Creator. They will realize further that no man need fail because he has failed to accumulate riches or greatness.

This is the golden age, and we are the most wonderful race of men that ever existed. Yet, in considering our achievements, we do not pay proper attention to our faults. Future races of Americans will not neglect this. In the coming days, when the winds will whisper and the birds sing over our graves, men will talk less of pessimism and optimism. They will speak more of the candid truth, with which the interests of the people are always connected.

Henry
George

The Last Man Must Have Land For His Standing Place

This ardent economist and reformer stood at the height of his popularity in the early 1890s. Henry George (1839-1897) had been born in Philadelphia, but his formal schooling was scant. At 14 he worked as an errand boy, and he went to sea (1855) as a foremast boy, sailing to Australia and India. Upon returning to America, Henry became a typesetter and remained in the printing/publishing field the rest of his life.

In 1858 George reached San Francisco, California. Including short stays in Oregon and Sacramento, the young man experienced several years of abject poverty— a situation shared with his young wife and two newborn children. In the depths of these depressed times, George began to form his theories of economic evolution. His early writings show one question to be basic to his thought: Why did social and economic progress have its twin in poverty?

Finally George became editor of the newly formed Oakland Transcript (1868). With this relative financial stability, he began writing articles and pamphlets to explain his economic theories, based on land tenure and land values. He modified these interpretations on the basis of the Panic of 1873 and its ensuing depression. Finally, in 1879, initial copies of his monumental Progress and Poverty were printed.

George moved to New York City in 1880 and his career as a propagandist began. An accomplished lecturer who drew huge crowds, Henry toured the British Isles and Australia to promulgate his views. He worked also as a newspaper correspondent and as an author of magazine articles. Soon he published The Irish Land Question (1881), Social Problems (1883), and Protection or Free Trade (1886)—while founding the weekly Standard (1887), devoted to his cause. Throughout the nation and in the

*British Empire, George encouraged the organization of scores of Land and Labor Clubs
to further the movement.*

*Keyed to the doctrine of the "Single Tax" (a levy on landowners that would fund
government and would free industry from taxes),
George's proposals gained widespread support among
liberal intellectuals and laborers. He ran an unsuccessful campaign for mayor of New York City
in 1886, and he was campaigning for the same
office in 1897 when he collapsed and died.
The tenets of George's economic thought are
contained in his brief comments on the
American future.*

Of all the questions you suggest as
to the changes that another century will
bring in the conditions of our people, one
is fundamental. That question, upon which
all the rest are dependent, is: "Will the tendency toward the accumulation of wealth in the
hands of a few increase or diminish?" While this
as yet can only be answered with an "if," the determining element is clear, for
it depends on laws as certain as that of gravitation.

By virtue of his physical constitution, man is a land animal. He is bound
by the necessities of his existence to the surface of the globe. On it he must live,
and from it he must draw for all his needs. No discovery, or invention, or improvement can rid him of this dependence.

The last man, as the first man, must have land for his standing place. He
must draw his subsistence, his very flesh and blood, from land. No matter how
elaborate, how refined, how potent his methods of production may become, they
must always have land as their indispensable basis and reservoir. Those methods must always consist in the combination of the matter and forces to be found
only in land.

This being the case, the fundamental social relation—that which determines
all others—must be, in the future, what experience shows it to have been in the
past: the tenure of land. Where the equal rights of all men to the use of land are
accorded, no serious inequality in the distribution of wealth can arise in peaceful
states. Here an advance in productive power will increase the general well-being
and lead to further advances.

But where land is treated as the property of some, from whom others must
purchase the privilege of living and working, a tendency to inequality is at once

set up. Here every advance in productive power tends to increase that inequality. For, since land is indispensable to the exertion of labor, no advance in the power of production can benefit those who have merely the power to labor.

That of itself being useless, the growth of population and the improvement of the arts can only drive the disinherited class of mere laborers into a fiercer competition with each other for the privilege of working. Meanwhile a larger and larger share of the production of labor passes into the hands of those who, in their monopolization of the natural element of all production, have control of the right to work.

Thus discovery, invention, and improvement—everything, in short, in which the material progress of society consists—tends under this primary injustice to increase inequality in the distribution of wealth. At last the monstrous inequality destroys advance and brings retrogression. Then, either in violent catastrophe or in dull dry-rot, inventions and discoveries are lost and arts and letters forgotten.

To us of the Western world—and especially to us of that New World which Columbus opened to European civilization—the wonderful improvements of the century now closing seem naturally but the prelude to far greater improvements in the next. However, we must not forget that the majority of the human race know nothing of our improvements.

Further, we must remember that the long history of humanity shows that advance has never before been continuous. And already we may see the growth of that inequality that has, over and over again in the world's history, stopped invention and improvement and has turned progress into decline. It is evident in the massing of monstrous fortunes on the one hand, and in the increasing intensity of the struggle to live on the other.

Nor is there anything that can check this tendency to inequality—save the recognition of equal rights to the use of that element from which alone men can live. Abolish all other monopolies save that of land. Still the ultimate result must be only to increase the share of the production of wealth that can be taken by land owners. Such an abolition cannot raise wages or make it easier for mere laborers to live.

Further, neither diffusion of education, nor purification of government, nor doing away with middlemen will prevent the widening of the gulf between the rich and the poor. This disparity must increase so long as land is treated as subject to that individual right of property that rightfully belongs to the things that human exertion brings into being. As to charity, that is hopeless. And it is worse than hopeless when not based on justice.

Therefore it is that the conditions which will exist in this country in 1993—when the children of children yet to be born celebrate the fifth centenary of the discovery of the great Genoese—must depend upon a single decision. That determination is whether, while they yet have power, the masses of our people accept or reject the one great reform which is embodied in the single-tax proposition.

If they accept it, and I now believe they will, then the Twentieth Century may see the development of a civilization that transcends the imagination of the Nineteenth Century. If they reject it, then there must befall us—but on a far grander scale and with a far quicker movement—what befell ancient Rome.

Annie
Besant

Brotherly Cooperation And Social Reform

Annie Wood Besant (1847-1933) remains one of the most unusual and interesting personages of her time. Born and raised in England, Annie—from the ages of 8 to 15— boarded with her tutor and remained separated from her family. At 20 she married traditionalist clergyman Frank Besant, with whom she had two children. When the marriage failed (1873), both children remained with the father—since Annie had become an active Free Thinker, the co-editor of the National Reformer, *and an adamant lecturer on birth control and population limitation.*

Thereafter Annie Besant progressed (1883) to the Socialist movement. She subsequently organized a labor strike to benefit exploited girls working in an English match factory. She also devoted much time, money, and organizational effort to programs that assisted London's wayward children and homeless girls.

In the late 1880s, Besant joined the Theosophical Society and became an ardent follower of Madame Helena Blavatsky—rising to the position of her first assistant. This movement proposed to establish direct contact with divine principle through contemplation and revelation, and thereby to gain a spiritual insight superior to empirical knowledge. When Blatvatsky died (1891), Besant succeeded her as head of the Esoteric School. She served as president of the Society from 1907 to her death.

In 1894 Besant removed to India and immersed herself in that country's nationalist movement. Her position proved so extreme that she was interned by the British government during World War I. She also promoted a young Hindu, Krishnamurti, as the "new Messiah," and travelled widely with him to raise funds for Indian nationalism.

To her death in Madras, India, at the age of 86, Annie Besant remained an iconoclast. She wrote voluminously—more than 100 books and pamphlets—and excelled as a propagandist, whatever her current cause. Besant's most interesting work may be her Autobiography (1893).

Regarding the civilization of the Western world in the light of the esoteric philosophy: I judge it a success or a failure as it approaches toward or recedes from the ideal of brotherhood; as it encourages or thwarts the spiritual progress of man. At present there are several causes, among many others, that are producing a state of social tension which must result in social change—peaceful or otherwise:

—The rapid increase of wealth in the hands of a comparatively small class;

—The growing control of natural forces by ever-widening knowledge;

—The exclusion of vast numbers of the population from the benefits of this growing control;

—The advancing education of the laboring classes and their ever-improving methods of combination.

It is against brotherhood that millionaires and starving men and women should coexist in society. It is against brotherhood that the growing control of natural forces should make the few scandalously rich, and leave the many scandalously poor. A society based on unbrotherly competition, instead of on brotherly co-operation, cannot last any more than can last a building built in defiance of the laws of mechanics. Hence I regard our present social system as doomed to collapse—as other systems have collapsed which were open to the same criticism.

Another reason for regarding this system as doomed is that it is an anachronism in conflict with the present stage of the evolutionary law. We are in the fifth great stage of human development, and the fifth stage is that of the mind. The function of man just now is to evolve the principle of intelligence dwelling within him. The mind powers already evolved give him sufficient control over physical forces to supply his bodily necessities and to leave him ample leisure for cultivating his intellect. It is time that this control be used for the general good, instead of for the heaping up of unnecessary wealth in the hands of a limited number.

The majority of our population, especially in the older countries—the European states—toil with little intermission all their lives, merely to keep life in their bodies. They have no leisure for cultivating the intellectual powers, the artistic faculties, or the imaginative potencies of the human mind. They are condemned to a life of labor—the price of which merely purchases them the right to live.

Thus does the horse earn his food and his shelter. Additionally, the horse receives generally more consideration for his health than is bestowed on his fellow drudge, the man who drives him. The horse needs but food, shelter, and rest. The man needs, for his human evolution, leisure for mental study with an unwearied body. That is the right of each child of man born into the world at this stage of evolution. Our animal development lies behind us. Our present task is to evolve the human element in us—the mind or soul.

Society should, therefore, be organized for the production of wealth with

the least possible expenditure of human energy and with the brotherly distribution of the wealth produced. Thus man's forces may be directed to the mental
development of the race. Our society sets itself against the order of evolution—
by shutting the majority of its members away from the possibility of performing
the task set them by nature. Such a society must be crushed under the relentless and irresistible progress of that nature which it blindly opposes.

While America has not yet touched the worst conditions of labor, found
so plentifully in Europe, its social organization is instinct—with the same forces
and, therefore, ultimately with the same effects. But being younger and stronger than the European states, it has more possibility of working out fundamental
reforms in peace than Europe seems to possess.

In the society of the future, it seems to me that the sexes will co-operate
for mutual service. Each will bring its special powers to the help of the race, without
artificial restrictions on either. In the future, a marriage entered into without
intellectual and moral affinities will be condemned as prostitution is now. And
marriage will be permanent, as intellectual and moral character is permanent.

In this future society, brutal crime will have disappeared. Subtler evils will
be met by brotherly compassion, not by vindictive penalty. Temperance legislation will be unknown because drunkenness will be as impossible as the readoption
of the woad garments of our ancestors.

In the future—ah, me! But I am thinking of a state much further in the future
than the America of 1993.

AGRICULTURAL BUILDING.

COPYRIGHT 1891.
THE WINTERS ART LITHO CO.,

John J. Carty

New Developments In Electricity Are Enormous

The career of electrical engineer John Joseph Carty (1861-1932) represents the immense impact that applied science made on Nineteenth-century American life. Carty was born in Cambridge, Massachusetts, and never entered college. Rather, he became so enthusiastic about the possibilities of the telephone that he joined the Bell Telephone Company in Boston (1879). Carty's inherent research and organizational skills proved so exceptional that he rose immediately through the fledgling company's ranks. In 1887 he became head of the cable department of the Western Electric Company of New York City and supervised scores of important cable-laying projects in the East.

As a researcher, Carty's motto became "Pick out a first-class difficulty and overcome it." His ability to perceive the essentials of a problem and to formulate simply and accurately the nature of the answer simplified countless research problems at Bell. Carty himself solved three problems hindering telephone development by inventing the "common battery," creating the high-resistance-bridging signal bell, and identifying cross interference in cables.

Just as important, however, were Carty's abilities as a corporate organizer. He became chief engineer of the Metropolitan Telephone and Telegraph Company (1889) in New York and completely revamped the company's equipment, methods, and technical work. In 1907 he performed a similar feat on the technical forces at the American Telephone and Telegraph Company.

During World War I, Carty successfully supervised all of the communications networking for the American Expeditionary Force troops in France. The military honors heaped on him were exceeded only by the myriad civilian awards he received prior to his death. In 1932 the American Academy of Sciences voted this pioneer the first re-

cipient of the Carty Award, established by AT&T to honor technical excellence and problem solving. No one deserved it more.

The probable developments in electricity in the Twentieth Century are almost inconceivable. We cannot tell what the next century may develop. If progress is as swift as it has been since Professor [Alexander Graham] Bell demonstrated that the human voice can be conveyed over a wire charged with electricity [1876], we are likely to see, early in the next century, some developments that will be simply revolutionary. Without suggesting any that may be regarded as merely the dream of a visionary or as the fanciful flight of imagination, I think perhaps I can indicate some developments that may be reasonably expected from present conditions.

In the first place, there is the use of electricity in domestic economy. I am inclined to think that not many years hence it will be found serving the household exactly as gas, steam, and coal now serve it. It will be possible for the cook, for instance, by simply turning on the electric current, to procure heat sufficient for all cooking purposes. When the cooking is done the electric current will be turned off. Thus there will be no wastage, as is the case now in the use of coal. Already there are electric cooking ranges in existence. I presume that these will be so highly developed that they will serve the most exacting requirements of a $10,000 chef.

Then, too, we may reasonably expect to see, at least in the cities, electricity used generally for heating purposes. That will also be an economy. There will be no wastage of coal. A single room may be heated by turning on the current, or a whole house, or a great building if that be the desire. It will also be used for lighting, I think, very generally. Its convenience and safety are now demonstrated. While it may not entirely supplant gas, it is certainly bound to be quite as widely used in private families as gas is now.

I think that the most important development, however—so far as domestic economy is concerned—will be found in a change in the manner of utilization of coal. In the larger towns, I presume that there will be no delivery of coal at the houses, as is now the case. Coal will be taken to a central station and there converted into electric energy, exactly as is the case now in the manufacture of gas. This central agency will furnish the electric current for heating, lighting, and cooking purposes. The economy will be very great. The wastage of coal is enormous, even in private houses. Since this is for the most part unavoidable, the general use of electricity for domestic purposes will be found to be an economy.

It is possible (although I do not want to be quoted as saying that it is probable) that, during the next century, the secret of the extraction of energy which is in coal direct may be discovered. If that is done, it will simply revolutionize civilization. It will vastly cheapen not only the cost of living, but the cost of all commercial enterprises. A very great percentage of the energy stored up in coal is now wasted. It goes forth through chimneys; it is lost in heat which is not utilized. The warmth which you feel when you go into a boiler room or into a kitchen is simply dead waste.

It has been estimated that, if the energy which is in coal could *all* be utilized, one ton would serve the purpose for which five tons are now required. This might give us possibly a solution of aerial navigation. It certainly would vastly cheapen traffic. It is almost impossible to estimate the consequences to civilization which might follow this discovery. I do not want to give the impression that I think the discovery will be made in the next century, but I am entirely willing to say that it is possible that we may hear of it at any time.

The remarkable discoveries of Nicola Tesla are going to play an important part, I think, in the commercial development of the next century. Tesla has discovered that an electric current (generated in a certain manner too technical here to explain) may be passed from one conductor to another, without any intermediary connection, like a wire. It will go through a stone wall precisely as light goes through glass.

The possibilities which lie in this discovery are simply enormous. And they may revolutionize some forms of development. For instance, it may have a powerful influence in the conduct of the wars that break out in the Twentieth Century, if any do. If it is possible to convey the electric current from one disk to another in a room without any medium, then it might be possible to direct it from a proper motor upon shore to the iron sides of a great war vessel. This might be done with such intensity as instantly to melt the iron or steel plates, as though they had been struck by lightning.

The use of the flashlight and the great electric reflectors is sure to be very general in military operations in the next century. And some of my acquaintances have sometimes suggested—not wholly in a flippant spirit—that electricity itself may be the great destructive agent employed in military operations in the Twentieth Century.

But more practical than this suggestion is another which is perfectly reasonable. I am inclined to think that the development of the trolley railway is going to be one of the mightiest factors in the urban civilization of the next century. The indications now are that it may solve some of the problems of overcrowding which have vexed the social economists. And, on the other hand, it may give to those who live in rural districts just that relief and recreation of which they are now deprived and which they so greatly desire.

I suspect that the trolley railway will be found extending from the hearts of our great cities far out into the country districts and over the highways. It then would be possible for a man to step from his front yard—or a farmer to go from his driveway—directly into one of these cars and, at the rate of 20 miles an hour or thereabouts, be conveyed to the city.

The passenger will not be obliged to bother about timetables. The cars will run with frequency and at trifling expense. They are simply going to annihilate distance and to make the man who lives in the country, to all intents and purposes, an inhabitant of the nearest city. It is easy to see what an important effect this will have upon the problems of great municipalities.

E. J.
Edwards

Journalism Is Pivotal In Man's Conquest Of The Elements

In the early stages of the "Age of Technology," Elisha Jay Edwards (1847-1924) proved one of the more vocal proponents of science as the key to American develop-ment. Born in Norwich, Connecticut, Elisha was 16 when his family moved to New Haven. He graduated from Yale University (1870) and the Yale Law School (1872) before attaining the Connecticut bar and establishing a law practice in town.

Edwards' interests, however, really rested in journalism and, in 1877, he joined the staff of the New York Sun. He served as the Washington, D.C., correspondent for the Sun (1880-1884) and the editor of the Evening Sun (1887-1890). He then became the New York City correspondent for the Philadelphia Press and, for the next 34 years, wrote a daily column under the name of "Holland" for the Press. Between 1908 and 1924, Edwards' column was syndicated to scores of newspapers across the nation.

Edwards most enjoyed investigative journalism. For example, in 1894, he broke the international "Sugar Trust" scandal, which led to a Senate investigation, conspiracy charges, and subsequent convictions. Throughout Edwards' writings, a consistent theme is his emphasis on science as the key to America's future.

The conquest of the elements, so that they may be made to serve mankind, is manifestly to be continued in the next century. That has been the distinguishing feature of the Nineteenth Century. How far men will subdue the forces of na-ture and compel service from them within the next 100 years is inconceivable. It is as unfathomable as it would have been for the men who fought the battles of the Revolution to understand how it could be possible to exchange intelligence with Europe on the instant, or to chat understandingly with a friend 1,000 miles away.

The destiny of the Twentieth Century is plainly the higher and more majestic development of man's joy and comfort of the secret, unseen powers that control the movements of the earth. These powers, which now operate by what are called nature's laws, cause the fields to blossom, the trees to bud and leaf, the storms to come, and the rain to fall. None of these things do we esteem marvelous because we are used to them—yet they give to this earth its life.

It is to be the province of journalism to report these mighty works of man and perhaps to stimulate them. When 100 years have passed, the newspapers will have made the world, if not kin, at least neighbors.

It is quite within the bounds of possibility that, by the year 1993, the mechanical work of publishing newspapers may be done entirely by electricity. The distributing of the printed papers also may be accomplished with such celerity as to vastly extend the legitimate field of any given journal.

It is quite possible that, by the agency of forces just beginning to be understood, the reporter and editor will no longer be compelled to write. Rather, the spoken word may appear imprisoned in cold type.

In one respect, the newspaper of 1993 will differ but little from that of today. It may report news with greater accuracy of statement, and it may have the world and its doings more completely subject to instantaneous report. But the newspaper of 1993 must be as is the newspaper of today—nothing but the story of human achievement, and the story of human nature, and the story of the happenings of earth. The object of the business of journalism cannot change. However, the methods of the business and its future development are likely to share the benefits which are to come from the mighty struggle of man with the elements to subdue them to his use.

Edwin
Checkley

Marked Changes In Medicine, Theology, Education

The field of medicine remained in a relatively primitive state in the 1890s. Both scientists and physicians fought epidemic diseases, while the family doctor addressed himself to major accidents, childbirth, and the alleviation of pain with drugs. The holistic approach of Edwin Checkley (1847-1911) attempted to integrate mind and body in the pursuit of exemplary health.

Edwin Checkley was born and educated in upper New York State, graduating from common school during the Civil War. In the 1870s he studied with a series of physicians in New England and began to develop his own philosophy of medicine. Checkley's system of "physiculture" slowly gained a local following, and he moved to New York City in the late 1880s to expand that audience.

His work entitled A Natural Method of Physical Training *(1890) spread Checkley's fame across the country. The volume underwent numerous revisions and printings, well into the 1920s. To teach "the Checkley System," the physical culturist also founded a school in New York City. It drew thousands of followers to a program of readings and exercise, until the cult leader's death in 1911.*

It gives me much satisfaction to predict that a marked change will take place in the science of medicine. By 1993 doctors will prescribe no more than one-third of the drugs they now think necessary. The true relation of the muscular system to the organic system, and their combined influence on the nervous system, will become more fully and generally understood. The combined action of the patient's mind and muscles will be depended on instead of drugs to prevent, allay, and cure disease.

In theology more change will be manifest in practice than in preaching—though sermons, too, will be different. Ministers will instruct their hearers in the philosophy of pure morality and teach them how to live. The government of the body by intelligent reason will be the one virtue inculcated. Ignorance and laziness will be the sins condemned and punished. The man who does not know how to keep his own body in health will be considered as great a sinner as the man who cannot read and write.

In methods of education there will be, in my judgment, marked changes. The tendency will be to return to the methods of the old Greeks—a slight practical idea of which can be obtained in any lecture room of one of our medical colleges. Instruction will be given orally. The practicing of the lessons will be done anywhere and everywhere. Children will be allowed to play or study as they please.

The veto power that teachers now exercise over children leaving the room during school hours will be taken from them. School children will have a playground instead of a yard for recreative purposes. And they will not be made to walk around it in lockstep manner. They will rather be incited to romp, shout, and play.

"Physical culture," so termed, I call physical destruction, and it will not be taught. A knowledge of how to breathe, sit, stand, stoop, walk, and run will comprise all the physical training that is necessary—and even that will not be forced on children under 15 years old.

Their physical training will come rather from their parents than from their teachers. To cover the whole field of education, in brief, the reasoning faculties will be developed instead of the memorizing ones. And hairline writing, along with children in spectacles, will be among the things of the past.

Mary E.
Lease

Improvements So Extraordinary The World Will Shudder

Raised a Roman Catholic, Mary Elizabeth Clyens Lease (1853-1933) parlayed her professional radicalism into the dismissal of all of her traditional beliefs. Mary was born in Pennsylvania and raised in New York. Prior to the Civil War, the family relocated to Kansas. Here Mary graduated from a Catholic academy and married (1873) Charles L. Lease, a local pharmacist. After moves within Kansas and to Texas, the Lease family (by this time including four children) returned to Wichita in 1883.

By 1885 Mary Lease had been admitted to the Kansas bar and had become a public and political figure. In 1888 she addressed the state convention of the Union Labor Party, and in 1890 she delivered some 160 speeches in behalf of the Farmers' Alliance–People's Party campaign in the state. When the Populists gained power, Lease was appointed president of the Kansas Board of Charities.

Mary Lease represented Kansas in several capacities at the World's Columbian Exposition in Chicago (1893)—where she delivered the keynote speech on "Kansas Day." Shortly thereafter she moved to New York to write political columns for Joseph Pulitzer's New York World. Lease's social campaigns included woman suffrage, prohibition, evolution, birth control, Roosevelt Progressivism, and the abolition of poverty.

Mary's strengths were her fervent public addresses, her translation of emotion to words, and her coining of picturesque campaign phrases. It was Mary Lease who admonished Kansas farmers in 1890 to "raise less corn and more hell!" Criticized for a lack of consistency, Lease nevertheless remained an iconoclast whose example greatly benefited American society at the turn of the century.

Victor Hugo, whose birthday France has made a national holiday, prophesying of the future, said: "In the Twentieth Century, war will be dead! Royalty
will be dead! Famine will be dead! But the people will live! For all humanity there
will be but one country, that country the whole earth; for all the people one hope,
that hope all heaven!"

When we contemplate the wonderful advances made by the world in the
past 50 years—the triumphs of skill, the
inventions of genius perfected and
brought about through the forces of steam
and electricity—imagination runs riot,
and the brain grows dizzy at the possibilities of the next century. We remember
that humanity is like blind Orion, struggling beneath his load to meet the God
of day: it finally has turned its face toward the light.

Humanity now is struggling toward
the realms of thought, developing a higher
intellectuality, progressing in an age of
ideas. We may well exclaim, "Ear hath
not heard, eye hath not seen, nor hath it entered into the heart of man," the
wonders, changes and gigantic progression that science, now in its infancy, hath
in store for the children of men.

In 100 years, the political and social improvements of the United States and
of the whole world will be so marked—in contrast with the social cannibalism
and pitiful wage slavery of today—that the world will shudder as it reviews our
time. The declaration of American independence will be the only political platform,
its inspiration the golden rule.

The map of Europe will be changed. Crowns will fail and thrones will crumble.
The divine right of kings and the divine right of capital will be recognized as
subterfuges, whereby the vicious and the idle lived upon the toil of others. The
reign of justice will be inaugurated.

The complexity of government will disappear—for the intricate and bur-
densome laws that now obstruct justice and bewilder and beswindle the masses shall be obliterated. The rule of the individual action will be the fullest liberty and the highest good of each, compatible with the fullest liberty and the
highest good of all.

The railroads, the channels of communication, light, water, and all public improvements will be managed by the state, in the interest of the people, and
owned by the general government. That superstition of a darker past (a fetich

[sic] taught by selfish partisans and college-bred idiots) that gold should be the basis of money, will disappear. It cannot stand before the full knowledge of the fact that a gold basis for a monetary system was a trick of the money breeders, to make money scarce and dear and to make both flesh and blood cheap.

Temperance legislation will consist in every man being a prohibitory law unto himself. In this way only can that evil, which is so deeply rooted in the human heart that legislation cannot reach it, be controlled and subdued.

With the amelioration of poverty, through the just distributions of the enormous profits of labor and the bounteous gifts of God, the per cent of criminals will be reduced to the minimum. The few who fall into evil-doing will do so because of the brute in the family blood that should have been subdued in their grand-fathers. To these individuals, the state will bring all the machinery of humane power to defend and improve—just as it now brings its power of law to prose-cute and brutalize.

With individual freedom and with the absolute right of the whole people to the free use of the earth and its resources, slavery and inequality will disap-pear. One sex will have equal opportunities with the other. Woman's depen-dence—the primal cause of man's brutality and sex slavery—will have become a thing of the past. Marriage will be not so much a contract of flesh, legalized for a fee, as a union of soul sanctified by an approving conscience.

The tendency toward the accumulation of great wealth in the hands of a few will decrease in the next century. The quickened conscience and the aroused conceptions of justice of an intelligent people will class the hoarder with the criminal who holds more of the world's gifts than he can possibly use, while his fellow beings want. The bounties of God shall not be fettered by the dead, but the earth and the fullness thereof shall belong in usufruct to the living.

Great corporations and business combines, which constitute the power of plutocracy, shall be controlled and dominated by nationalism—the creature shall not be greater than its creator. With a government "of, for, and by the people," in fact as well as tradition, the condition of the laboring classes will be one of comfort and independence.

Three hours will constitute a long day's work. And this will liberally fur-nish infinitely more of the benefits of civilization and the comforts of life than 16 hours' slavish toil will provide today.

Opportunity will thus be given to improve and develop those God-given faculties and aspirations that lie dormant in every human soul. Books and music, athletic games, and mental and physical culture will occupy the time and thoughts of a healthy, happy, godlike people—who will send out thought messages from soul to soul, from place to place, as an arrow flies from the bow of the archer.

Agriculture will be developed by electricity, the motive power of the future. Science will take, in condensed form from the rich loam of earth, the life force or germs now found in the heart of the corn, in the kernel of the wheat, and in the luscious juice of the fruits. A small phial of this life from the fertile bosom of Mother Earth will furnish man with subsistence for days. And thus the problems of cooks and cooking will be solved.

The slaughter of animals—the appetite for flesh meat that has left the world reeking with blood and bestialized humanity—will be one of the shuddering horrors of the past. Slaughter houses, butcher shops, and cattle pens will be converted into conservatories and beds of bloom. Man and beast will hold life sacred. And the vegetarians of the next century will exclaim with [Oliver] Goldsmith:

> No flocks that range the valleys free,
> To slaughter I condemn;
> Taught by that power that pities me,
> I learn to pity them.

The dress of the future will offer no resistance to, or compression of, action. Bathing ever in the infinite ocean of good, the "house beautiful" will not be prematurely decayed by sickness, distorted by pain, or racked by fashion's tortures. Vulgarity will not conceal or expose. "To the pure all things will be pure." The practice of the maxim "Know thyself" will make the body honored and resplendent—"the temple of the Holy Ghost."

The race will be mentally and physically healthier, happier, and handsomer because the mothers of the race—no longer dependent upon man—will be freed from his bestiality. Meanwhile man's animality will decrease in proportion to the increase of his mentality. Woman shall have the sole right to say when she shall wear the crown of motherhood. Thus our jails and almshouses, our streets and alleys shall no longer swarm with the spawn of degraded men.

Improvements, inventions, and startling discoveries will so crowd and supersede one another that our limited human ken cannot today grasp them all. We will tear down the barriers between the seen and the unseen and hold converse with the disembodied. We will travel over land and water and through the air by means of electricity. We will hold communication with the inhabitants of other planets, and Sunday excursions to the mountains of the moon will not excite comment.

The center of population has moved westward 500 miles in the past century. Judging the future by the past, the greatest city will be located on our boundless Western prairies. Here the almond-eyed Mongolian from the Orient will meet, in the tide of humanity pouring westward, the Aryan brother from whom he separated on the plains of Asia 6,000 years ago.

Where Chicago now lifts her proud spires and many-storied buildings, a great lake of inland seas will surge its restless waters. The dwellers on its banks will tell, with bated breath, of the cataclysm that engulfed the doomed city and rolled the waters upon its sin and pride.

The American now living who will be the most honored in 1993 will be that man who is today endeavoring to exemplify in his life and teachings the spirit and doctrine of Jesus Christ. It will be he who is lifting from the rubbish of the temple the book of books—he who is leaving nothing undone to bring about that time of which Isaiah sung and the prophets have so long foretold. Unhonored by wealth or station, though not unknown, this American lives today for his fellow men, beloved by all who meet him. The ripest years of his white manhood he has been writing justice on the nation's page. And this shall be his sure reward, for "With what measure you mete unto others, it shall be meted unto you."

> For ever the truth comes uppermost,
> As round and round we run;
> And over the right shall triumph,
> And ever shall justice be done.
> Yours for the kingdom coming...

GALLERY OF FINE ARTS.

COPYRIGHT 1891,
THE WINTERS ART LITHO CO., CHICAGO

Albert D.
Shaw

Buffalo-Hamilton-Niagara Falls: Greatest Manufacturing Center In The World

Albert Duane Shaw (1841-1901) was born in Lyme, New York, and educated at St. Lawrence University. He served with the 35th New York Volunteers during the Civil War and returned to Watertown to be elected to the New York Assembly (1867). A most effective Republican orator, Shaw was appointed the U.S. Consul at Toronto (1868), where he served for almost a decade.

In 1878 the diplomat was promoted to a similar post in Manchester, England. During the next seven years, Shaw built a reputation among the English for his veracity, propriety, and kindness. Shaw's reports to the U.S. State Department were notable for their perceptive comments on foreign manufactures and on potential tariff and revenue reform.

Upon his retirement from the foreign service (1888), Albert Shaw became the president of the Canadian Niagara Power Company and later the New York Commander-in-Chief of the Grand Army of the Republic. In the former capacity, he was particularly well-informed on the subject of a future megalopolis in the Buffalo area.

One of the greatest cities in the United States will be found to occupy the area between Buffalo and Niagara Falls. I think that, early in the century, there will be a city of 1,000,000 inhabitants there. It will be one of the greatest manufacturing cities in the world. It will include practically the City of Buffalo, as well as the towns upon the borders of the Niagara River.

This great city is to be developed through the capturing of the power of Niagara Falls, which even today is practically consummated—and which, from the time of the discovery of this country, has gone to waste. This water power is to be mainly utilized in the development of electricity. And both the Canadian and the American falls are to be made to serve this purpose.

A power will be developed there sufficient not only to run all the engines necessary to turn the wheels in as many factories as can be located in this area.

But it also will be sufficient to furnish the City of Buffalo with light and with electricity for domestic uses. Further, I am inclined to think that this complex may even provide power and light for cities as far away as New York and Philadelphia on the east and Cleveland, Cincinnati, and Toledo on the west. The capacity here is practically limitless.

Even with the great plants now established on the American side and with those contemplated on the Canadian side, only a comparatively small portion of this enormous power is being utilized. It has the advantage of being not only cheap, but permanent. No drought will ever affect the Niagara Falls. And the cost of furnishing power will not be dependent upon the operations of capitalists who control the coal fields.

Already there are indications of the growth of this city. Manufacturers from all parts of the United States are securing rights there. Even before the close of this century we shall see a considerable city established there. Early in the next century, I look to see a continuous manufacturing city extending from the Niagara River to what are now the outskirts of the City of Buffalo.

Nature has done everything to favor this locality. At last science and capital are taking advantage of these natural temptations. My own opinion is that, during the next century, this will become the greatest manufacturing center in the world. Men now in the prime of life will see enough, I think, to justify me in this prediction—and before many years have passed.

Junius Henri
Browne

Simplification And Cooperation

The journalist Junius Henri Browne (1833-1902) was born in New York but raised in Cincinnati, where he received his education at St. Xavier College (1849). At 16 years of age he began work in his father's banking house, but left it at 18 to pursue a career in journalism. He wrote for several Cincinnati papers and then, when the Civil War commenced, he contracted as a war correspondent for the New York Tribune.

Captured by Confederates near Vicksburg in 1863, Browne spent almost two years being shifted from prison to prison. In 1864 he escaped from the Confederate prison in Salisbury, North Carolina, and traveled 400 miles through enemy territory before reaching Union lines. Browne tells of his experiences naively in Four Years in Secessia *(1865).*

After the war Browne returned to New York City and became a member of the editorial staff of the Tribune *and later of the* New York Times. *He also frequently served as a New York City–based correspondent for other newspapers and wrote books on such diverse subjects as the French Revolution and life in the City. Browne gained a reputation among his peers as an astute observer of the American scene—on many levels.*

I am, and have always been, a great believer in America and everything American. The form of government is ideal. It will, no doubt, meet the requirements of its citizens for generations, if not for ages, to come.

The social and political condition of the country in 1993 will be, in my opinion, a marked improvement on what it is now. It will tend more and more to humanity, reason, freedom, and independence of the individual. Socialism, which is in the air, will steadily grow here in a modified and rationalized form. There will be more equality in education, position, and fortune.

The republic will be more than ever democratized. The government will be simpler. The railroads and telegraphs will in all probability be owned by the state and managed excellently—better than they have been at any previous time.

Legislation on the subject of temperance will be more enlightened. There will be no attempt to enforce total abstinence, but there will be less drinking and far fewer rumshops. Those that are permitted will be obliged to pay very high license and will be thoroughly regulated by law.

Criminals will be less severely punished and their number will have materially diminished. General education will have greatly lessened crime.

The divorce laws will be the same in all the states. Divorce will be freer generally than at present. But it will be allowed for only a few moral causes—among them non-support, disloyalty, crime, intemperance, and temperamental incompatibility.

Wealth will be more widely and equally distributed. Great corporations and business interests will be conducted harmoniously—on the principle of the employers and workers sharing in the profits. The conflict between labor and capital will be largely settled in this way, aided by cooperation. As a necessary result, the laboring classes will be much less dependent.

Food will be provided in the next century at a low cost and without difficulty for our entire population. Schemes to advance the prices of the necessities of life will have become so discouraged by public opinion as to be no longer practicable.

Law will be simplified. Lawyers will have diminished, and their fees will have been vastly curtailed. The principles of medicine will be more generally and intelligently understood. There will be much more dependence on nature than on drugs or physicians, who will have decreased.

Theology, as such, will be little taught and will have almost no influence. Authority will have no weight; faith, as respects dogma, will be without esteem. The doctrine then will be deed, not creed. The churches, outside of the Roman Catholic, will coalesce—will be as one. They will preach morality only and inculcate charity.

American literature will stand at the head of English literature. The drama will be its best and most accepted form.

The social and political status of women will be on a par with that of men. They will enjoy the elective franchise.

The servant problem will have adjusted itself to the needs of the community, and will have ceased to be an injustice and a torment to householders.

The race will be handsomer, healthier, and more contented—through increased education, knowledge of science, and human sympathy.

Samuel
Barton

The Wonderful Development Of Florida

In the world of American financial movers-and-shakers in the early 1890s, Samuel Barton (1827-1895) sat in the innermost circle. Barton was born on Staten Island to Colonel Samuel Barton, who sat in the New York State Assembly (1821-1822) and represented New York's First District in Congress (1835-1837). The boy's mother was a sister of "Commodore" Cornelius Vanderbilt (1794-1877), the steamship and railroad magnate who established the family fortune.

Samuel graduated from Harvard Law School (1848), attained the New York bar, and joined a New York City law firm. Commodore Vanderbilt favored Samuel and, in 1852, engaged him as cashier of his Atlantic Steamship Company. Shortly thereafter he became the Commodore's primary broker and served his uncle's financial realm with distinction, for he was named one of the executors of Vanderbilt's estate. In the 1860s and 1870s, Barton engineered some of the major stock and securities coups that marked the Vanderbilt empire, including the Erie Railroad takeover.

After 1877 Barton directed various Vanderbilt enterprises, ranging from numerous railroad lines to the Lincoln Bank to the Brooklyn Storage and Warehouse Company to the Lincoln Safe Deposit Company. Until his death, Samuel Barton remained the prime broker for Vanderbilt operations, working out of the J. W. Davis and Company firm. If Samuel Barton recommended investments in Florida in the early 1890s, one would be wise to heed his words.

It is my opinion that there is to be a wonderful development of the resources of the State of Florida in the next century. Our people do not understand what a magnificent territory that is. It will become not only the great sanitarium for the invalids of the East. But, in my opinion, it also will be a rival with Nice and other Mediterranean districts for those who seek pleasure and comfort in winter travel.

Already some of the capitalists who have been attracted to that Florida country are developing it by means of the railways. Before the beginning of the next century, a railroad will skirt the Atlantic shore almost as far down as the Florida keys. This great subtropical territory will be as thoroughly crisscrossed by railways as are some of the states of the North.

I think our pleasure-seekers will discover that the lower part of Florida has as many temptations in the winter season as have any of the winter resorts of Europe. I look to see the islands in the Caribbean sea become the resort of those who seek fashionable pleasures. For there they will find much greater natural beauties than are to be enjoyed on the shores of the Mediterranean—and there is none of those distressing mistrals which sometimes make life miserable at those Mediterranean resorts.

I doubt whether the lower part of Florida will ever be drained so as to make that section available for agriculture, although almost anything is going to be possible in the next century. Completely to drain that area would require the building of a ditch as deep and broad as the Mississippi River. Farther north, however, I think we shall find, early in the next century, that the great sugar belt there will be completely under cultivation. And it is capable of producing millions of pounds of sugar.

Transportation facilities will be so increased that the orange district, especially upon the east coast, will practically furnish the United States all the oranges the market requires. Pines and coconuts will be grown in southern Florida to such an extent as to command the markets of this country.

I think I am not making a wild prediction when I say that, in the next century, the value of Florida to the United States will be of more commercial importance than are some of the states in which even bonanza mines have been discovered.

David
Swing

Remarkable Progress Of The Nation Toward Purity

By the early 1890s, David Swing (1830-1894) had become an institution on the Chicago scene. Swing was born and raised in Ohio, graduating from Miami University (Oxford) in 1852. Although prepared as a Presbyterian minister, he returned to Miami to become a professor of Latin and Greek and to supervise its preparatory department. In 1866 he suddenly accepted a call to the Westminster Presbyterian Church in Chicago and preached there for eight years.

Theological purists charged Swing with heresy in 1874. Although he was exonerated, the minister resigned from the presbytery in 1875. Supporters then created the new downtown Central Church for Swing, with an immediate congregation of more than 500 persons. From this platform until his death, Swing preached to 2,000 to 3,000 each week. Through his published sermons, the clergyman reached tens of thousands more.

David Swing had become an editor of The Alliance in 1873 and, for a decade, it published one of his sermons each week. The (Chicago) Inter-Ocean and the Chicago Tribune likewise published a weekly sermon, expanding Swing's audience throughout the Midwest.

His writings, steeped in literary references, were prized for their originality, liberal spirit, and practical helpfulness. Swing published compilations of these sermons almost annually between 1874 and 1894. Admirers noted that this preacher was a devotee of beauty and had the mind of a poet, although he remained a pragmatist in practice.

It is almost certain that the United States will continue to advance in all the next 100 years. The sunshine, rain, and soil are constant quantities—in the sense that they seem quite secure for one more century. Coal oil and natural gas will no longer exist, but there will be plenty of wood and coal. There will be food for all, although the great West and Southwest will be settled as densely as Germany. By 1993 Mexico and Canada will be in the North American republic and will furnish homes for many new millions.

The American President will be elected for 6 or 8 years. He will not be eligible for a second term. Near the close of the next century, some rare, noble woman will be elected President of the United States.

Railways will be so leveled and straightened that slow freight trains will make 100 miles an hour. The best of passenger trains will run 130 miles an hour. It is not certain that steam will be the form of power. New powers are liable to be discovered. One cent per mile will be full fare.

Considerable traveling will be done by the air route. The fact that air is an ocean which will float a man settles the question of aerial navigation. Man has simply to invent the kind of boat. It must be very large and strong. It must come. This boat may be guided from city to city by a wire strung about 100 feet above ground, so as to let the balloon pass over trees and houses. Thus a wire one-quarter of an inch in diameter will hold and guide many balloons full of people.

On account of fast and cheap travel, cities will become groups of suburbs. Thus all the poor will have air, sunshine, and light. Suburban fare, 20 miles, will be two cents, on what are called "zone tickets."

The working people will all be shareholders in the farm or factory where they work. They will simply draw dividends. They also will lose by all strikes, because they will strike against their own interest.

Literature, the drama, and all life will be higher and purer—because the increase of common sense implies an increase of all that is good. Dress of woman will be simpler, and the conduct of man more honorable, for each 100 years makes man and woman less of a fool.

The Christian church will rest wholly upon the words and life of Christ. The writers of the Bible will stand related to Christ only as valuable forerunners and missionaries of the one great Chief. The church will be a vast impulse and guide in art, ethics, benevolence, and worship.

Great calamities will come in the form of pestilence, earthquakes, and civil strife, but they will not much impede the progress of the nation. [George] Washington and [Abraham] Lincoln will still be the most honored names—because no other two minds can again find two such tasks to be performed.

Ignatius
Donnelly

More Complex Political And Social Reform

During his lifetime, Ignatius Donnelly (1831-1901) wore many hats: farmer, politician, editor, orator, reformer, author. Born to Irish parents in Philadelphia, Donnelly received only a public-school education. Yet he read law and was admitted to the Pennsylvania bar in 1852. A trip to the Old Northwest then convinced the young man to abandon both the East and the law for land speculation in Minnesota. Here Donnelly established the somewhat-utopian community of Nininger. When the Panic of 1857 dashed his development, the entrepreneur turned his lots into wheat fields and thereafter considered himself a farmer.

Donnelly's penchant for oratory drew him into local politics during the pre-Civil War period, and he eagerly embraced the new Republican Party. He served as lieutenant governor of Minnesota (1859) and then was elected to three consecutive terms in the U.S. House of Representatives (1863-1869).

Donnelly offended party officials, however, and never returned to national office. He also renounced the Republicans and thereafter joined a series of third-party campaigns: Liberal Republican; Granger; Greenback; Farmers' Alliance; Populist. As this electrifying orator moved to more radical reform, he broadcast his views both from the lectern and through his reform weekly, the Anti-Monopolist (1874-1879).

Between 1870 and 1900, Donnelly served numerous terms in the Minnesota Legislature—under various party labels but always as a spokesman for radical reform. His greatest political recognition derived from his Populist affiliations in the early 1890s. The ringing preamble of the party's Omaha platform (1892) was entirely Donnelly's work, and he was the party's vice-presidential nominee that year. Critics, however, denounced the reformer as a "visionary" and the very "prince of cranks."

As an author, Donnelly proved equally unconventional. The unfailing wit and humor that made him such a popular speaker suffused his prose, but his subjects ranged from an argument for Atlantis as the source of civilization to an intricate explanation of Francis Bacon's authorship of William Shakespeare's works. In 1891 Donnelly published a very well-received futuristic novel, Caesar's Column; A Story of the Twentieth Century. *This work earned him the sobriquet of the "Sage of Nininger."*

Ignatius Donnelly wrote widely in American newspapers during the 1880s and 1890s. He also edited his own reform journal, The Representative, *and contributed regularly to such magazines as the* North American Review. *Including his political commitments in Minnesota and his speaking engagements around the country, Donnelly had created a national public presence by the end of the Nineteenth Century. Somewhat fittingly, he died on January 1, 1901—the first day of the Twentieth Century.*

Who can speak with any positiveness of anything in the time to come? Who can
> Look into the seeds of time
> And say which grain will grow and which will not?

There are seeds to which divinity seems to give especial and prodigious fructification, and others which—even as they sprout green and abundant—wither and disappear from the affairs of men.

Who could have foreseen 300 years ago that the little seed of liberty would expand into such a vast harvest and fill the world? Or who could have foreseen that the immense bonfires of religious intolerance which then blazed in all lands, with the blood trickling out from among the ashes, would subside into a few embers, spitting spiteful sparks while kicked aside by the foot of intelligence? And there may be obscure seeds among us today whose growth 100 years from now shall embower the nations.

The greatest event which has happened in the historical period to man on earth was the discovery of America. We have no means of estimating its far-reaching consequences, which will spread down the ages for 10,000 years, constantly expanding, intermingling with each other, and creating a million unexpected combinations. It means the transference of the highest civilization and the greatest races of men to a continental arena better fitted than any other on the globe for their unlimited development.

First we had a strip of settlements along the coast nearest to the parent source. Then we had an outbreak, growing out of abundant food, high spirits, and a semiwild hunter condition. Then came the creation of a nation—a copy, to a large extent, of the institutions of the country which gave us our language and laws. Then all the fountains were opened together, and every land in Europe poured confluent streams of population into the vast stomach of the woods and prairies. We now are digesting it all and creating a race and a people unlike anything that has existed before in the history of the world.

Our civil war was but a temporary incident growing out of local and temporary causes. It simply stirred up the mental activity of the population to a high pitch and made manifest, on both sides, the warlike and heroic characteristics of a mighty race.

Everything that is past is, however, insignificant compared with that which is to come. When we have 500,000,000 inhabitants, our civil war will be little more than Jack Cade's rebellion is to the Englishmen of today.

Of one thing we may be sure—that ours will be a vast world, whether existing under one government or many. Edmund Burke said that men "breed by the mouth"—signifying that the population of a country will be in proportion to its food supply. And, as we have the greatest agricultural area in the world, it follows that we will have a tremendous population, unless everything is swept away by social convulsions.

It is one of the astonishing puzzles of the past that the Indian race—being flanked on the south and southwest by a comparatively high civilization, setting up their tents amid the ruins of the race that built the mounds and forts of the Ohio Valley, and dwelling on the most productive soil on earth—nevertheless were arrested in numbers and development. Thus, after thousands of years of occupancy, the land was almost uninhabited. It would certainly seem as if some extra mundane power had held the red man in check and reserved the continent for the use of the white man.

The government will grow more complex. All development moves away from simplicity toward complexity. Man has more organs than the oyster. Nature began with a single cell and expanded into human civilization.

The first government was probably the simple and gentle patriarchal system. When the grandfather ruled, by the ties of love and duty, the group of his posterity assembled around his central tent. The ancient kingly government gave nothing in exchange for the plunder it took from the people, save protection from foreign hostility. Every step in the march of development has made the government more complex. The rights of the multitude had to be protected against the rights of the tyrant—hence customs, parliaments, laws, courts, police, etc.

Men object to "paternalism" in government, and yet they themselves share in the fatherly intervention of the state in a hundred particulars.

Government is simply the aggregated individuals protecting the individual. It not only enforces taxes from him as in the old time, it lights his streets, carries his letters, protects his person, watches over his property, securely keeps the title deeds to his real estate, furnishes him with water and light in his house, erects his schools, educates his children, builds his highways, assists him to move by rapid means of locomotion, protects him on the ocean, looks after him in foreign countries, excludes contagious diseases from his shores or stamps them out if they secure a footing, inoculates him against pestilences, establishes parks for his entertainment in the great cities, creates botanical and zoological gardens, hires musicians to delight his ears with pleasant sounds, secures him in the possession of liberty, counts his votes, punishes those who wrong or injure him, and helps him to collect the money due him. Govern-ment, in short, watches over him as no father in the world ever watched over his sons.

And there is not one of these particular aids that the citizen would vote to relinquish. He would as soon think of stripping off his clothes on a winter day as give up these advantages and comforts. Hence when men talk against "paternalism in government" or echo that threadbare sophism, "That country is governed best which is governed least," they prate against civilization and would turn the shadow back on the dial of time.

In other words, that progress to increased enjoyments for the many, which has been the marked feature of these later ages, has built up a multitude of new rights of which our barbarous ancestors knew nothing. And every one of these rights has to be protected by law against the brutality and rapacity of our fellow men. Hence, with every increase of human happiness there has got to be a further reaching out of human government.

Many of the evils of which we complain today are simply due to the fact that man's ingenuity has invented new forms of injustice—forms for which, as yet, no remedy has been devised by government. You can reconstruct the history of the race out of the statute book. Read the laws against murder, and they bring before you that ancient day when manslaughter was honorable and the highest accomplishment of the leading citizens of the community consisted in expeditiously dispatching their fellow creatures.

Read the law against larceny, and you recall the time when all property was in common. Read the law against adultery, and it carries you back to the era before the establishment of the institution of marriage. Read the Bill of Rights and, when it speaks of separation of church and state, the whole history of Europe for a thousand years passes before you like a terrible panorama of cruelty and bloodshed.

Strip the people of all these enactments, and you have nothing left but barbarians.

And in the future this process of state intervention will continue. It will increase until the aggregate man (called government) reaches into the affairs of all the citizens and protects every right and secures every blessing which our material limitations will permit us to enjoy during this strange, earthly career. For, like the swallow in the old Saxon story, we simply dart out of the darkness, flash through the light, and disappear into the darkness beyond—enjoying only one momentary speck and fragment of life.

"Is it likely that the railroads and telegraphs will be owned or managed by the state?"

The world 50 years from now will laugh at the picture which the historian will give of this era—when a free people permitted excrescences to grow out of themselves to suck their substance.

A railway is simply a highway. It is a public road. If it were not so, the property of private parties could not be condemned to build it. The state can take private property for public use. It cannot take private property for private use. A railroad is a highway with a tramway to decrease friction, and steam substituted for horsepower. It is a testimony to the shortsightedness of the race that these public roads were ever permitted to pass into the hands of individuals or corporations. Who would advocate today placing our wagon roads under the control of a company or association, thus preventing all other parties from using them?

It is very evident that the time is not far distant when the people will repossess themselves of the iron highways. They will be compelled to do so in self-defense. As it is today, the railroad corporations (to protect their "watered stock" and their pooling combinations, formed to prevent competition) are forced to interfere in politics, dictate the selection of governors, congressmen, and United States senators, corrupt legislatures and pick out the judges of our courts. These practices are fundamentally destructive of representative government. They lead inevitably to universal rottenness, out of which must come armed revolution as a last, desperate remedy.

Communication by electricity is simply an improvement upon communication by mounted couriers, stagecoaches, and steam cars. The Morse alphabet is only a substitute for the common alphabet. If the state is justified in taking charge of the mails, it is equally justified in taking charge of this aerial communication carried on the wings of the lightning.

Concerning our monetary system, I would simply make a suggestion or two.

We boast that we have passed beyond the barbarous system of barter in which the Eskimos and other rude races still remain. This is a mistake. The whole monetary system of the civilized world is still based on the barter of two metals—gold and silver—which have come down to us as precious metals from prehistoric times, in which they were sacred metals, dedicated to the worship of the sun and moon. When England ships gold to the United States, or vice versa, the nation simply repeats the "swapping" of that metal for commodities which the Phoenicians carried on along the Mediterranean coasts 5,000 years ago, or which Christopher Columbus practiced 400 years ago with the Indians of Central America.

The use of gold and silver as the basis of the world's commerce is not, therefore, the result of the wise selection of a congress of highly civilized nations, but simply the perpetuation into the cultured present of a barbarous custom drawn from the remote past. And the money classes of the world are now trying to discontinue the use of one of these prehistoric mediums of exchange. They are trying to rest the whole business of a rapidly expanding civilization upon a metal of which there is in the world about enough to form a cube 24 feet square, and which is being absorbed in the arts of Europe alone at the rate of $24,000,000 per annum.

Can lines

Finite one way be infinite the other?

Can mankind advance chained to this clog? Can the population, wealth, and business of the world expand indefinitely in every direction—while that which regulates prices is steadily decreasing in quantity and dragging down values, preventing prosperity, crippling enterprise, and creating innumerable paupers? Can the fate of all mankind depend upon a 24-foot cube of an accidental metal? Is not such a condition unworthy of the high civilization into which we are advancing?

What is the remedy? An international paper money which all the wealth of the world would back up and sustain legal tender among all nations. This paper money would be increased in precise ratio to the increase in population or wealth of the world.

Are not the financial troubles of today due largely to the conflict between the necessities of a vast development and the limitations of an ancient superstition? And is not this conflict likely to make the close of this century as revolutionary and bloody as the close of the last century?

William Jennings
Bryan

Government Nearer
To The People

Perhaps the signal politician of the late Nineteenth Century was William Jennings Bryan (1860-1925). He was born in Illinois and schooled in Jacksonville, where he graduated from Illinois College in 1881. Bryan was admitted to the bar in 1883 and had practiced for four years when he relocated in Lincoln, Nebraska. Although he built a fair practice there, Bryan abandoned the profession when he was drawn into politics—first as a successful Democratic candidate for the U.S. House of Representatives (1890).

After serving in Congress (1891-1895), Bryan returned to Omaha and became editor-in-chief of the Omaha World-Herald. He also began an extensive lecturing program, sometimes tied to the Chautauqua circuits, which allowed him intimately to encounter the opinions of the populace.

From these audiences, William Jennings Bryan discovered the political power of the free-coinage-of-silver issue. This theme (sometimes restated as the opposition of the people to the power of wealth) became the basis of his three national presidential campaigns in 1896, 1900, and 1908. The issue is most recognizable today in Bryan's "Cross of Gold" speech, delivered to the Democratic National Convention in Chicago in 1896.

A man of obvious personal integrity, seemingly endless energy, and a magnificent stage voice, Bryan dominated Democratic politics in the United States for more than two decades (1895-1915). His own newspaper, the Commoner (1901-1915), aided mightily in keeping Bryan's views before the public. Interestingly, he served President Woodrow Wilson as Secretary of State (1913-1915). From this position he converted his personal pacifism into almost 30 arbitration treaties with foreign powers.

A strong Presbyterian his whole life, Bryan advocated a literal interpretation of the Bible, and he opposed any of the evolutionary theories. For these reasons he was invited to join the prosecution team for the 1925 Scopes "Monkey Trial" in Tennessee.

At this trial, defense attorney Clarence Darrow called Bryan as a witness and conducted a blistering cross-examination. Five days following the conclusion of the trial, Bryan died quietly in his sleep.

The government will grow more complex perhaps in its details as increased numbers, greater area, and larger interests require more machinery—but it will grow more simple in purpose. Instead of seeking to perform the work of the individual, it will content itself with "restraining men from injuring one another." It will "leave them otherwise free to carry on their own pursuits of industry and improvement," so far as they do not interfere with the equal rights of others. Changed conditions will compel the government more carefully to guard the weak from the aggressions of the strong.

Free competition is not what it used to be. Trusts and combinations left uncontrolled have both the small dealer and the consumer at their mercy. The government must furnish a sure protection to the interests of all of the people from the cupidity of some of the people.

Much of the increasing inequality in wealth is due to laws absolutely unjust and to the absence of necessary restraining laws. We may not be able to destroy the natural disparity between men, but we must avoid exaggerating it by legislation. Political equality cannot exist long in the midst of great social and pecuniary inequality. There is an evident and growing desire to bring the government nearer to the people.

General education among the masses and improved facilities for spreading information have prepared the people for more complete participation in the work of self-government. We have outgrown the present method of electing senators by legislatures. The selection of those who are to represent us in our highest legislative body will soon be taken out of the hands of state representatives and placed in the hands of the people, where it belongs. The election of president by an electoral college—which often turns the contest on a few pivotal states and sometimes thwarts the will of the people—is destined to be replaced by a more direct method of ascertaining the popular will.

Shelby M.
Cullom

Government Should Never Own Modes Of Transportation Or Communication

As a 14-year member of the Senate Committee on Interstate Commerce, Shelby Moore Cullom (1829-1914) developed well-informed opinions on the nationalization of the country's railroads and telegraph lines. Cullom was born in Kentucky and moved as a child to a northern Illinois farm. Here he received an academic and university schooling, but then found reading law in Springfield preferable to frontier agriculture. He was admitted to the Illinois bar in 1855.

In the same year, Cullom was elected the Springfield city attorney, thus beginning what he termed "a political career exceeding in length of unbroken service that of any other public man in the country's history." An early member of the Republican Party, Cullom was elected a member of the Illinois State House (1856; 1860-1861, 1872-1875), a Representative in the U.S. Congress (1865-1871), the governor of Illinois (1876-1883), and U.S. Senator (1883-1913).

Cullom's primary political expertise involved the regulation of commerce between states. He was the driving force behind the creation of the Interstate Commerce Commission (1887), served as the chairman of the Senate Committee on Interstate Commerce for years, and directed through Congress the Hepburn Act (1906) concerning railroad regulation.

As a politician, Cullom was scrupulously honest and kept an open mind on issues—until he decided his position, which he then defended tenaciously. He was critical, but fair, in his judgment of men, and he proved a tireless political organizer and worker. Critics depicted Cullom as "colorless," perhaps because he entertained no vices. Nevertheless, *he was a Republican stalwart from the inception of the party until World War I—all in all, a remarkable politician.*

In my judgment, government ownership of the railways and the telegraphs would be the most serious blunder that this country could make. It would bring about a condition of things which would menace the peace and the very life of the republic. Government should regulate—but not own—railways and telegraphs and other concerns with which the commerce and prosperity of the people are so intimately connected.

Take the railways of the country alone, and you will find that they employ more than 1,000,000 men. This means not 1,000,000 citizens merely, but 1,000,000 voters. For these railway employees are not women or children, but men of voting age—men stalwart, alert, capable, skillful. You might say that they are a compact body of 1,000,000 picked men from all walks of life in this country, representing the flower and prime of our manhood.

It would, in my judgment, be monstrous to turn these men over to the control of the government and the manipulation of the politicians who might chance to be in power in that government. If these men were made vassals of the dominant party, there need never be a change of administration. The political party that could not maintain itself in power with this mighty engine at its command would be weaker than any political party we have ever yet had in control of the nation.

In addition to the men, there are the contracts for supplies, for construction, and for all the requirements of the vast railway lines. The money value of these contracts would run into figures beside which the expenditures of the government itself are as a mere bagatelle. Still more effective would be contracts for transportation, secret rebates, and favor in cars and facilities. These things are serious evils even as they now are. The people will never be satisfied, in my opinion, until they have suppressed such practices.

However, with railways in the hands of the government, favoritism in shipments and rates would be inevitable. Such favoritism would surely be used for political purposes. The maintenance in power of the dominant party by such means would bring other evils in its train. And the final result could be nothing less than open revolt, rebellion, revolution.

It is my solemn conviction that no man who loves his country should, for one moment, think of placing railways and telegraph lines in the ownership and control of the government.

Octavus
Cohen

Revolutionary Trends In Drama And Music

As a resident of South Carolina, Octavus Cohen (1860-1927) brought an unusual perspective to the traditional criticism of music and drama. Born in Montgomery, Alabama, Octavus was educated in Charleston schools and by tutors. As a young man, he travelled extensively in Europe, before returning to work on small papers in Cohoes, Troy, and Albany, New York.

Cohen moved to New York City in the early 1880s, where he edited the performing-arts department for the American Press Association, a national ready-print syndicate. For this market he wrote numerous pieces of art criticism over the names of "Crispin" and "Octy Cohen." Simultaneously Cohen read law in Saratoga County.

When Cohen returned to Charleston (1886), he continued his preparation for the bar, to which he was admitted in 1887. While establishing a new practice, he founded the (Charleston) Sunday Budget. This paper quickly proved financially success-ful, and Cohen created the Charleston Daily World. The World became the voice of South Carolina's agricultural-reform movement and was instrumental in the sur-prising election (1890) of many Populist candidates.

Besides his newspaper and law careers, Octavus Cohen wrote two opera librettos, two comedy-melodramas, a Southern play, and a high-grade drama depicting life in the Elizabethan age. His son, Octavus Roy Cohen (1891-1959), proved an even more prolific Southern writer. He authored scores of popular mysteries, adventures, and historical novels and developed an extensive national following.

By the time that the scroll bearing the legend "A.D. 1993" shall have been unfurled, the popular taste will demand in the drama much of the same mate-rial which served to delight our grandparents half a century ago. In other words, Shakespeare will be on top, and the nondescript fever and ague concoctions of the present day (called for want of a better name "sensational melodrama") will have passed away, together with the incongruous mixture of vaudeville, farce, and negro minstrelsy now known as farce comedy.

It is not to be supposed, however, that one class of entertainment will suffice for our great-grandchildren. While most of them will incline to the strictly legitimate, there will still be many who will want a different sort of amusement. The tastes of these people will be supplied by American dramas, with the comedy and tragic elements both strong.

These plays will, in a great measure, deal with the peculiarities of life in different sections of the country. They will be faithful pictures, for they will be written by residents of the various localities. The lighter form of theatrical entertainment will be farce, with songs which are germane to the story.

Music in America will have advanced marvelously. In 1993 there will be hundreds of persons with as fine voices and as excellent methods as [operatic coloratura soprano] Adelina Patti now possesses. But they will not be considered marvels and will be glad to receive as much per month as that favored lady is paid per night. Music of about the quality of "Il Trovatore," with dialogue instead of recitative, will be the vogue. Concert will be obsolete, as will also what we call "comic opera."

In music and the drama, the salaries of the ordinary performers will be smaller than now, owing to the increased purchasing power of money. Yet the few (possibly less than a dozen in the whole world) who may succeed in eclipsing all competitors will receive incomes which would dazzle [renowned French actress] Sarah Bernhardt and cause Adelina Patti to have convulsions.

The money which is now expended for elaborate scenery and gaudy costumes will be devoted to increasing the membership and efficiency of the company. America will, during the next century, produce worthy rivals of [Ludwig van] Beethoven, [Wolfgang Amadeus] Mozart, and [Giuseppe] Verdi, while in the drama [Richard Brinsley Butler] Sheridan and [Oliver] Goldsmith will be surpassed. Shakespeare's equal, simply as a writer of dramatic language, will never live.

Theaters for the better class of performances will be few in number for the reason that each reasonably well-to-do man (and there will be lots of them in 1993) will have a telephote [sic] in his residence. By means of this device, the entertainment at any place of amusement in that city may be seen as well as heard.

All theaters will have revolving stages, so that there will not be more that 10 seconds' wait between acts. This will, of course, do away with the vile orchestras which now torture us.

The chairs will not be arranged in rows, but will be divided off into little stalls, with an aisle on each side. Attached to each chair will be a call bell, an opera glass which may be used without the formality of dropping a dime in the slot, a faucet from which ice water may be drawn, and a tumbler from which to drink the cooling beverage.

Theaters will be illuminated from outside, mirrors bringing the light of softened and even form into the building. The footlights will be small calciums of different colors. Performances will begin at 10 o'clock and end at midnight. Chicago will be the eastern headquarters of the theatrical world, and San Francisco the western.

Actors and singers of ordinary repute will be received into the very best society. Those of particularly great reputation will be eagerly sought after by fashion's leaders. Stock companies will have disappeared altogether, and no posters on the dead walls will there be in 1993.

HORTICULTURAL HALL

Hempstead
Washburne

Most Progress
Will Not Be Radical

At the time of the preparations for the World's Columbian Exposition in Chicago, Hempstead Washburne (1852-1918) served as the city's mayor. This progressive Republican derived from staunch stock. His father, Elihu B. Washburne (1816-1887), had been elected from Illinois to the U.S. Congress (1852-1868), had served a short term as President Ulysses S. Grant's Secretary of State (1869), and had performed heroically (1869-1877) as U.S. Ambassador to France, particularly during the Franco-Prussian War.

Hempstead was born in Galena, Illinois, and sent by his father to prep school at Kent's Hill, Maine. After graduation (1871), he joined his family in Europe and enrolled in the University of Bonn, Germany. After two years he returned to read law at the University of Wisconsin and, subsequently, at the Union College of Law in Chicago. After graduation (1875), the young man opened a law practice in Chicago, which became Trumbull, Washburne, and Robbins.

A faithful Republican, Washburne was appointed Master in Chancery of the Cook County Supreme Court (1880-1884), and then he was elected City Attorney for Chicago (1885-1889). He won a five-way race for the mayor's post in 1889 by a mere 369 votes, yet Hempstead proved one of the city's most progressive leaders.

During his two years in office, not only was the Chicago's South Side infrastructure improved substantially in preparation for the World's Columbian Exposition, but other reforms occurred: the establishment of a juvenile court system; the construction of an elevated-train system; the restriction of public gambling; the abatement of smoke; the development of a pure-water system; the systematic institution of a street-sanitation program; the creation of public bathing beaches. This tenure established Chicago as the leading progressive urban center in the Midwest.

After his term as mayor, Washburne engaged in the banking business, managed *his father's estate, and developed an outstanding law practice. He remained a staunch Republican, engaging in many Illinois party activities, and involved himself in scores of local civic projects. The "Mayor who put on the Fair" always held opinions on a wide array of topics.*

The political condition of the United States in 1993 will be very similar to that of the present. Its social development will evolve a less ostentatious display of wealth. This will result from the increased intelligence and the education of the masses—who even now frown upon unseemly displays of wealth as evidencing exceedingly bad taste.

The government, if then in existence, will become more simple, both in methods of election and in its executive branches.

Railroads, telegraphs, and other quasi-public corporations will either be owned by the government or be under its control.

Our monetary system will doubtless be upon a gold basis, solely owing to the increasing output of silver and copper.

Temperance legislation will doubtless assume the form of high license and local option. Sumptuary prohibitory laws will not be countenanced by any intelligent and independent people.

There will be little if any change in the confinement or punishment of criminals—excepting that places of confinement will be conducted under more stringent supervision and all buildings made more in conformity with sanitary rules.

Divorce laws will still be maintained. Marriage relations will continue about as they have for the last 1,900 years.

The accumulation of wealth will increase in the hands of individuals, until some time in the future. Then laws will be enacted to regulate the amount of wealth which may be inherited. In other words, laws will seek not to restrict the accumulation of wealth by the individual, but will restrict his leaving the same intact—so as to prevent the creation of a moneyed aristocracy by inheritance.

The future of great corporations and business aggregations will tend toward more perfect centralization, until the monopolies become so obnoxious that they will be regulated by federal and local statutes.

The laboring classes will doubtless become thoroughly organized, and thereby attain a position of more independence as a body. The so-called laboring classes of today, when properly organized in the future, will compose the great bulk of the conservative wealth. They will produce population and will doubtless be so regulated by the laws of union as to eliminate worthless characters.

When this is attained, the entire union of the laboring class will compose a certain middle class. The third social class will be composed principally of those who are unfitted by moral habits from entering the labor ranks.

I look forward to union labor as the backbone of the republic in the next century. It will be to posterity what the well-to-do New England farmer and mechanic was to the past and is to the present age—neither rich nor poor, but sufficiently rich to be independent and educated.

The agricultural resources of our country, by comparison with Europe and older civilizations, are such as to justify the belief that the country will be able to care for its population (no matter how great) for many centuries yet to come.

The changes in law will keep pace with the requirements of the people and will grow with the civilization, as in the past. Theology will doubtless liberalize and broaden to meet the advanced thought of that age.

In a century from this time, without doubt, there will have been established a purely American literature as distinctive as that of any other old country of -today. Music and the drama will doubtless follow the literature of the day.

The educational methods will advance with the growing intelligence of the people. The standard education of today will doubtless be looked back upon with as much contempt as we look back upon the average education of a century ago.

Dress will doubtless be similar to that of today, with some reform in the line of health in the dress of women.

Architecture and sanitary arrangements will doubtless be improved, by virtue of new methods and new discoveries, to a point which we do not as yet dream of. Transportation in great cities will be solved by some new genius who is yet unborn. The problem is one of so much moment that all minds are turned to this question, and as yet no perfect solution has been discovered.

It is not improbable that women may obtain the right of franchise in many states. Her social status will then, as now, be what she herself makes it.

The servant problem will doubtless keep pace with the rheumatism, gout, and other evils incidental to humanity, as long as servants exist.

It is as useless to attempt to foretell the improvements in mechanics, in industrial arts, and in modes of travel as it would have been 40 years ago for any one to have anticipated the telephone and its now universal use.

The race will doubtless be handsomer, and it will be more refined in its general makeup and manners. Perhaps the race will be not so healthy, for it will drift more toward sedentary habits. And perhaps it will not be any happier, because of the greater struggle then for existence, caused by the greater competition.

Following history—which shows that the great cities of every continent are inland cities—Chicago or some inland city will be the largest in the United States.

Walter
Wellman

Revolutionary Improvements In Transportation

Walter Wellman (1858-1934) was an adventurer and a journalist, in that order, and he was particularly well-versed in transportation developments. Wellman was born in Ohio and received a district-school education in Michigan. At the age of 14, he started a weekly newspaper in Sutton, Nebraska. At 21 he founded the Cincinnati Evening Post. *From 1884 to 1911 he worked as the political and Washington, D.C., correspondent for the* Chicago Herald *and its successor, the* Record-Herald.

As an adventurer, Wellman first tasted national publicity when he journeyed to the Bahama Islands (1891) and located the "exact spot" where Christopher Columbus landed on San Salvador (Watling Island). He erected a monument to this location, just in time for the Columbian quadcentennial and the World's Columbian Exposition in Chicago (1893).

Wellman also made several unsuccessful assaults—overland and by air—on the North Pole in 1894, 1898-1899, 1906-1907, and 1909. His most remarkable adventure, however, involved an attempt to cross the Atlantic Ocean by airship in 1910. Although the balloon crashed into the ocean, the flight set a record for time (72 hours) and distance (ca. 1,080 miles), and for the first time wireless messages were transmitted from land to an airship over water.

In the early 1890s, Walter Wellman was living closer to the future than most Americans. In addition to his writing and adventuring, he worked as an expert consultant on urban rapid-transit projects. Thus his observations on man and transportation prove most perceptive.

The thought of what our civilization will be, will have, and will know 100 years hence is fascinating. In all the prescient horizon, there is nothing that captivates the imagination so completely as the means of travel which mankind will invent, create, and evolve. I am neither an engineer nor an inventor. Yet I think I see that we are on the eve of improvements and departures in travel which will, in the space of 50 or at most 100 years, amount to revolution.

Improvements in steam locomotives (already made and tried) indicate that very soon—with corresponding improvements in tracks and carriages—speeds of 80 to 100 miles per hour on long runs will be commonplace. As the speeds increase, luxuriousness will increase also. The appointments of parlor and sleeping coaches could not be much finer than they are. But means will be found to prevent or to reduce the oscillation and jarring movement of the best coaches. Then one may ride at 100 miles an hour in such quiet that he will scarcely know, from his physical sensations, that he is flying through space.

The electrical railway will, probably within 10 years, carry its travelers at a much higher rate of speed than this. Then the principal trunk lines between east and west, north and south, will run trains at 150 or more miles an hour. Not only will these lines elevate the tracks to secure clear way, but they also will enclose them with light structures of glass or other material to escape atmospheric impediment.

Steam railways will be extended to the uttermost parts of the continent, from Alaska to Patagonia. While this extension is going on, new and simpler forms of electric railways will enable all populous rural regions to enjoy the benefits of rapid transit and cheaper transportation. Individual farmers will have their own lines for the movement of products to the main line.

For letters there will be a postal telegraph, cheap and in almost universal use. There will also be electrical postal lines, carrying mail matter across the continent at a speed of 200 or 300 miles an hour. Morning newspapers in all the large cities will be delivered at the breakfast tables of their readers by this means, within a radius of 500 miles of the office of publication.

Moreover, man will perfect the system of extracting from the earth the terrestrial magnetism with which it is impregnated—that is, electricity. This system will make that power cheap and common. In the utilization of electricity, we shall have electric carriages, wagons, delivery carts, and bicycles.

Aerial navigation will come within the next century. It may not become universal or largely commercial, but it will be used for special travel, for exploration, for pleasure. It will be accomplished not by balloons—since a balloon that floats in the air cannot be steered at will. Rather, it will be realized by the aeroplane, in combination with stored electric energy, operating through engines of marvelous power and lightness. Within 25 years, aerial navigation will solve the mystery of the North Pole and the frozen ocean.

The most important improvement in the means of travel—the one which will work greatest good to mankind—will be in metropolitan rapid transit. This is the greatest field today for the engineer and inventor. The solution of the problem, in my opinion, will be found not in underground railways—which are never likely to become popular in America. Rather, it will be found in elevated electric railways, enclosed with glass.

Take that greatest of American thoroughfares, Broadway, for instance. It runs from one end to the other of the greatest metropolitan-residential district on this continent. One hundred years hence, it will be a scientific street.

Over each sidewalk, on a level with the first story of the buildings, will be an enclosed way of glass—securely closed in winter, partly open in summer. Through this will run two lines of cars in the same direction. One line will move at a speed of 30 or 40 miles an hour and will never stop, except in case of emergency. To and from these through-trains, passengers will be shifted by using movable platforms, also operated by electricity.

A brief explanation will make the idea clear. At the Twenty-third Street Station, many passengers are waiting to proceed downtown. Several cars come to rest by the station platform. The passengers step aboard. In one minute they are moving southward at a rate of 30 miles an hour. Gates are thrown open. They step from the platform cars to the cars of a train moving on a parallel track at the same speed.

At the same time, the passengers who wish to leave the through-train at the next station pass from the train to the platform cars. They pass out at the station, when these cars come to a rest there a few moments later. At this station the platform cars serve as at the Twenty-third Street Station, and so on down the line. During the moment of transfer, to and from the movable platforms, the two trains are interlocked and moving at the same speed. Stepping from one to the other, therefore, is as easy as stepping from a stationary platform to a train at rest.

By this method every passenger uses what is to him a through-train. Without any delay whatever, he passes from the way- or local-train to the fastest train on the through line. Automatic speed-governing devices will make collisions impossible and will permit trains on the through-line to be run one minute apart. Each train will have a capacity of 500 or 1,000 passengers. This will give a carrying capacity of from 30,000 to 60,000 passengers per hour in each direction over one line.

If traffic warrants, the through-trains may be made continuous. The result would be virtually a stream of people moving on either side of the thoroughfare, at great speed and in perfect comfort. The stations would be enclosed within the glass structure. And in winter or storm, there would be no discomfort from the elements in opening doors or passing to and fro.

The transparent structure would not darken the street or the adjacent buildings.

It could be made ornamental and artistic. Instead of disfiguring the thorough-fare, it would improve it aesthetically and practically. Pedestrians underneath would find a roof over their heads—keeping off rain and snow and making it possible for the crossings to be kept clear of mud and detritus.

Better still, the space between the structures and the buildings could be con-verted into an elevated sidewalk. Thus the second stories of shops, opening upon this arcade, would be as attractive as the lower ones. The convenience and capacity of the buildings would be increased at the same time that the street below would be relieved of its congestion.

In my opinion, the elevated and enclosed electric metropolitan railway will solve the rapid-transit problem. The system offers a roof for present sidewalks and an arcade for second-story entrances; it features continuously moving trains served by movable platforms. Thus will be alleviated the rapid-transit problem in New York, Chicago, Boston, and other chief cities in the republic, long be-fore the new century shall have waned.

J. P.
Dolliver

The Purpose
Of Wealth Is
A Divine Purpose

Even in an age of self-made men, Jonathan Prentiss Dolliver (1858-1910) proved exceptional. He was born in West Virginia to a family that moved from the woods to Morgantown so Jonathan could obtain a quality education. He graduated from the University of West Virginia (1876) and—after some footloose travelling in the Midwest— read for the law and was admitted to the West Virginia bar in 1878.

At the age of 20, Dolliver determined to launch his legal practice in Iowa, and he located in Fort Dodge. Although his career developed slowly, his remarkable oratorical abilities led him into the state's Republican politics. Taking conservative, agrarian stands on national issues, Dolliver was elected to six successive terms in the U.S. House of Representatives (1889-1901). In 1900 he was appointed to complete one of Iowa's Senate terms, and was reelected twice to the seat (1900-1913).

Politically Jonathan Dolliver moved gradually to more liberal positions. He also rose to real power within the Congress—sitting on the pivotal House Ways and Means Committee and chairing the influential Senate committees on education and labor, as well as agriculture and forestry. These positions provided the energetic Dolliver a ready platform for his oratorical prowess. Never a wealthy man himself, Senator Dolliver understood the role that wealth played in the American scheme.

The most interesting tendency of these times is toward the use of great estates for the general welfare. The next century, while it may see the limitation of estates, will in nowise consent to the destruction of the right of individual ownership.

The most influential forces at work in the field of social economy are moral and spiritual. It is becoming evident, even to profane eyes, that the world is a

Purpose and not a Mass. A century can get much out of that view of things, unless it goes stone blind.

It can, for example, secure a restatement of the real motives of living and, thereby, possibly bring mankind back to the strongholds of the early faith. It is not by accident that the past 50 years, a half century of incredible progress, have seen the accumulation of money on a scale hitherto unheard of in the world. It has experienced not only the piling up of individual possessions, but also the general increment of wealth in every modern state. The bearing of a worldwide phenomenon like that is not truly discerned by those who, in the wealth of individuals, see only a standing threat against the commonwealth.

Already there are signs that the purpose of wealth is a divine purpose. Thus thoughtful hearts, often cast down in the presence of the vulgar ostentation of riches, may take courage. Every day the press records the gift of thousands, often of millions, to public enterprises. The last week of the last December poured into the channels of education, charity, and religion more than $5,000,000.

What does it signify when a single Christmas is made memorable by such farsighted philanthropy as that of Philip D. Armour and John D. Rockefeller? It is a hint of the coming era, when all wealth—in order to escape reproach, if for no higher reason—shall enlist itself in the volunteer service of civilization.

A thousand enterprises looking to the progress of the human race are crippled by the want of money. A hundred splendid little American colleges are struggling with the problem of poverty. The church, in all her branches, seeking to move along the broad lines of the gospel, finds her magnificent projects at home and abroad belittled and discredited by a narrow treasury.

It is as sure as any future thing that the making of money—or, more properly, the accumulation of money—is to go on through the coming century. Nor does it take a very acute insight to perceive that we are approaching a time that will not be defined by reforms proposed by state socialism. Rather, during this time, the products of labor, the fruits of genius, the dividends of investment, and the spoils of commerce shall be more and more willingly put aside in the generous plans of the rich as trust funds, involving a high stewardship, for the ultimate use of the community.

Henry V.
Boynton

The South As Manufacturing Empire

By the early 1890s, American leaders were exhorting the citizenry to redirect their attention from the Civil War and its aftermath to the country's exciting involvement in the industrial revolution. One of the journalists who eased this transition was Henry Van Ness Boynton (1835-1905), a Civil War hero himself.

Boynton was born in West Stockbridge, Massachusetts, but removed to Ohio in his boyhood. He graduated from Woodward College (1854) in Cincinnati and from the Kentucky Military Institute (1858). During the Civil War, Boynton rose to the rank of major and then lieutenant colonel in the 35th Ohio Volunteer Infantry.

A born leader, Henry Boynton commanded regiments in the battle of Chickamauga and in the storming of Missionary Ridge. He was breveted brigadier-general for gallantry at Chickamauga and Chattanooga, and he was awarded the Congressional Medal of Honor for his actions at Missionary Ridge.

After the war, Boynton became a popular newspaper correspondent in Washington, D.C.—a position he held to the turn of the century. His two best-known books are Sherman's Historical Raid (1875) and The Chickamauga National Military Park (1892). Moreover, Henry Boynton wrote regularly, knowledgeably, and with compassion of the South's evolution in the post-war period.

Very frequent visits to the South during recent years lead me to believe that the greatest development of the next century will be in that section. During the last decade, for the first time in its history, the South has roused itself to a comprehension of its limitless resources.

The war was a blessing, both to the nation and to the South. The abolition of slavery was not its chief good. That was an incident. The emancipation of the white race was its greatest boon. Labor has been dignified; industry and energy are striding to the front and into leadership. Cotton was king, negro labor cultivated it, and iron and coal and the other abounding resources of a great empire slept almost unknown and undeveloped. Now agriculture is diversified; mines are pouring out their wealth; the hum of varied manufacturing is the music of the new time.

The Piedmont region of the South will, long before the next Columbian centennial, be the New England of the new South. This is the region of the Appalachian ranges and their foothills, from the Potomac to central Georgia and Alabama. It includes West Virginia, eastern Kentucky and Tennessee, northern Alabama and Georgia, western South Carolina, western North Carolina, and a large portion of old Virginia. It is 500 miles long and 200 miles wide. Its wealth in minerals, coal, and all that the hills, mountains, and forests produce is beyond computation.

Railroads have just rendered all this accessible. The South's surface resources, which alone as yet are known, plainly indicate inexhaustible wealth. It has a climate which cannot be surpassed in the temperate regions. Its short winters are not only most attractive, but constitute an important element in development—since seasons for outdoor work are longer, and the needs of clothing, fuel, and stock feeding are far less.

These uplands afford unlimited pasture and are everywhere adapted to grain and fruit. The streams are abundant, and water power is inexhaustible. In its streams, its hill country, and its mountains, the South is a magnified New England, while its southern climate gives it superior advantages.

Before the next centennial, the South will be the empire manufacturing region of the continent. The rich lowlands surrounding it will find consumers there for its products. The mountain and hill resources, the manufacturing population (reducing and transforming them into the uses of civilization), and the supporting lower countries together will form mighty communities—of which the new life now everywhere throbbing through this wonderful region gives certain promise.

J. H.
Beadle

All Prophecy Is Futile

The journalist and author John Hanson Beadle (1840-1897) became the obvious choice to write the closing piece in the American Press Association's series forecasting North American life at the end of the Twentieth Century. For he worked as a contract writer for the APA and carried a broad background of general knowledge.

Beadle was born in Indiana and, after some public schooling, he enlisted in the 31st Indiana Infantry to serve in the Civil War. Discharged in 1862 for disability, he entered the State University of Michigan and studied law in addition to his liberal-arts course.

After graduation (1867), Beadle opened a law practice, but quickly abandoned it for a career in journalism. He signed on with the Cincinnati Commercial and became its prime correspondent from the American West. In the course of his Western travels, Beadle worked for one year as the editor of the Salt Lake City Reporter—after which he wrote his most popular work, Life in Utah; or, The Mysteries and Crimes of Mormonism *(1870).*

Beadle's other successful books also were set in the American West and relied on his experiences there during the late 1860s and 1870s. In the 1880s, however, he developed a widespread following as a writer of editorials and historical/political articles for the APA. John Beadle's years of practical experience obviously rendered him a logical observer of "the futility of prophesy."

The spirit of prophecy is abroad, and the futility of modern prophecy is beautifully illustrated almost daily. This era is singularly prolific of books like [Ignatius Donnelly's] *Caesar's Column* and [Edward Bellamy's] *Looking Backward*, with minor articles in which the future is portrayed. One radical philanthropist has given us a painfully interesting work, based on the tenth census [1880], to prove that the negroes will soon predominate in eight states. Another futurist has proved to his own satisfaction that Christianity cannot outlast the Twentieth Century, and many others promise us many other wonderful things.

Of all these forecasts, one thing may be said with tolerable certainty: Not one of them will be verified in its essential details. All history goes to show that the progress of society has invariably been on lines quite different from those laid down in advance, and generally by reason of inventions and discoveries which few or none had expected.

Since mankind advanced so far as to have a literature these forecasts have been a favorite amusement with talented men of certain ideal temperament. Plato's ideal republic and Sir Thomas More's Utopia are prominent instances. And it is a fact, and a most significant fact, that from Plato down the whole line to Dr. John Cumming every such guess at the future has been made ridiculous by the actual facts.

The explanation is simple. The prophet is compelled to judge from the forces in operation in his time, and the wisest man cannot possibly foresee the results of the next invention. So far from expecting the railroad and telegraph, Plato and Thomas More could not possibly have comprehended such things if revealed to them by one divinely inspired. [U.S. Senator Henry W.] Blair, [political analyst Albion Winegar] Tourgee, and many more had scarcely proved to us what would happen in the South, on the basis of the tenth census, when the eleventh census [1890] showed us that the whites there were increasing much more rapidly than the blacks.

"Don't never prophesy unless y'know," was the sensible advice of a backwoods statesman, and it is peculiarly appropriate just now. The present evil, say the present prophets, is the concentration of wealth, the growth of corporate power, and the disproportionate increase of city populations. But it is possible—nay, it is quite probable—that the next invention will be of a method of storing energy, so it can be shipped in small packages and applied wherever wanted.

In that case, Niagara Falls may supply power to run the manufactories of Texas. Power can be applied on a small scale just as economically as on a large scale, and every little town—every rural neighborhood perhaps—can have its little cotton and woolen mill. The farmer may plow his fields and heat his dwelling with a storage battery no bigger than a common brick, and the coal monopoly will be as dead as Julius Caesar.

But, on second thought, this is prophesying. And that must be cut short.

Populations of U.S. States & Territories: 1890 & 1990

	1890	1990
Alabama	1,513,017	4,040,587
Alaska	—	550,043
Arizona	59,620	3,665,228
Arkansas	1,128,179	2,350,725
California	1,208,130	29,760,021
Colorado	412,198	3,294,394
Connecticut	746,258	3,287,116
Delaware	168,493	666,168
District of Columbia	230,392	606,900
Florida	391,422	12,937,926
Georgia	1,837,353	6,478,216
Hawaii	—	1,108,229
Idaho	84,385	1,006,749
Illinois	3,826,351	11,430,602
Indiana	2,192,404	5,544,159
Iowa	1,911,896	2,776,755
Kansas	1,427,096	2,477,574
Kentucky	1,858,635	3,685,296
Louisiana	1,118,587	4,219,973
Maine	661,086	1,227,928
Maryland	1,042,390	4,781,468
Massachusetts	2,238,943	6,016,425
Michigan	2,093,889	9,295,297
Minnesota	1,301,826	4,375,099
Mississippi	1,289,600	2,572,216
Missouri	2,679,184	5,117,073
Montana	132,159	799,065
Nebraska	1,058,910	1,578,385
Nevada	45,761	1,201,833
New Hampshire	376,530	1,109,252
New Jersey	1,444,933	7,730,188
New Mexico	153,593	1,515,069
New York	5,997,853	17,990,455
North Carolina	1,617,947	6,628,637
North Dakota	182,719	638,800
Ohio	3,672,316	10,847,115
Oklahoma	61,834	3,145,585
Oregon	313,767	2,842,321
Pennsylvania	5,258,014	11,881,643
Rhode Island	345,506	1,003,464
South Carolina	1,151,149	3,486,703
South Dakota	328,808	696,004
Tennessee	1,767,518	4,877,185
Texas	2,235,523	16,986,510
Utah	207,905	1,722,850
Vermont	332,422	562,758
Virginia	1,655,980	6,187,358
Washington	349,390	4,866,692
West Virginia	762,794	1,793,477
Wisconsin	1,686,880	4,891,769
Wyoming	60,705	453,588
United States	62,622,250	248,709,873

Sources: U.S. Department of the Interior, Census Office, *Report on Population of the United States at the Eleventh Census: 1890.* Part I, p. 2. Washington, D.C.: G.P.O.; 1895. Also U.S. Department of Commerce, Bureau of the Census, *Final Report: Population of States of the Union.* Reprinted in: *World Almanac and Book of Facts, 1992.* New York: Scripps Howard; 1991.

100 Most Populous Cities In The United States: 1890

1.	New York, New York	1,515,301	51.	Lynn, Massachusetts	55,727
2.	Chicago, Illinois	1,099,850	52.	Lincoln, Nebraska	55,154
3.	Philadelphia, Pennsylvania	1,046,964	53.	Charleston, South Carolina	54,955
4.	Brooklyn, New York	806,343	54.	Hartford, Connecticut	53,230
5.	St. Louis, Missouri	451,770	55.	St. Joseph, Missouri	52,324
6.	Boston, Massachusetts	448,477	56.	Evansville, Indiana	50,756
7.	Baltimore, Maryland	434,439	57.	Los Angeles, California	50,395
8.	San Francisco, California	298,997	58.	Des Moines, Iowa	50,093
9.	Cincinnati, Ohio	296,908	59.	Bridgeport, Connecticut	48,866
10.	Cleveland, Ohio	261,353	60.	Oakland, California	48,682
11.	Buffalo, New York	255,664	61.	Portland, Oregon	46,385
12.	New Orleans, Louisiana	242,039	62.	Saginaw, Michigan	46,322
13.	Pittsburgh, Pennsylvania	238,617	63.	Salt Lake City, Utah	44,843
14.	Washington, D.C.	230,392	64.	Lawrence, Massachusetts	44,654
15.	Detroit, Michigan	205,876	65.	Springfield, Massachusetts	44,179
16.	Milwaukee, Wisconsin	204,468	66.	Manchester, New Hampshire	44,126
17.	Newark, New Jersey	181,830	67.	Utica, New York	44,007
18.	Minneapolis, Minnesota	164,738	68.	Hoboken, New Jersey	43,648
19.	Jersey City, New Jersey	163,003	69.	Savannah, Georgia	43,189
20.	Louisville, Kentucky	161,129	70.	Seattle, Washington	42,837
21.	Omaha, Nebraska	140,452	71.	Peoria, Illinois	41,024
22.	Rochester, New York	133,896	72.	New Bedford, Massachusetts	40,733
23.	St. Paul, Minnesota	133,156	73.	Erie, Pennsylvania	40,634
24.	Kansas City, Missouri	132,716	74.	Somerville, Massachusetts	40,152
25.	Providence, Rhode Island	132,146	75.	Harrisburg, Pennsylvania	39,385
26.	Denver, Colorado	106,713	76.	Kansas City, Kansas	38,316
27.	Indianapolis, Indiana	105,436	77.	Dallas, Texas	38,067
28.	Allegheny, Pennsylvania	105,287	78.	Sioux City, Iowa	37,806
29.	Albany, New York	94,923	79.	Elizabeth, New Jersey	37,764
30.	Columbus, Ohio	88,150	80.	Wilkes Barre, Pennsylvania	37,718
31.	Syracuse, New York	88,143	81.	San Antonio, Texas	37,673
32.	Worcester, Massachusetts	84,655	82.	Covington, Kentucky	37,371
33.	Toledo, Ohio	81,434	83.	Portland, Maine	36,425
34.	Richmond, Virginia	81,388	84.	Tacoma, Washington	36,006
35.	New Haven, Connecticut	81,298	85.	Holyoke, Massachusetts	35,637
36.	Paterson, New Jersey	78,347	86.	Fort Wayne, Indiana	35,393
37.	Lowell, Massachusetts	77,696	87.	Binghamton, New York	35,005
38.	Nashville, Tennessee	76,168	88.	Norfolk, Virginia	34,871
39.	Scranton, Pennsylvania	75,215	89.	Wheeling, West Virginia	34,522
40.	Fall River, Massachusetts	74,398	90.	Augusta, Georgia	33,300
41.	Cambridge, Massachusetts	70,028	91.	Youngstown, Ohio	33,220
42.	Atlanta, Georgia	65,533	92.	Duluth, Minnesota	33,115
43.	Memphis, Tennessee	64,495	93.	Yonkers, New York	32,033
44.	Wilmington, Delaware	61,431	94.	Lancaster, Pennsylvania	32,011
45.	Dayton, Ohio	61,220	95.	Springfield, Ohio	31,895
46.	Troy, New York	60,956	96.	Quincy, Illinois	31,494
47.	Grand Rapids, Michigan	60,278	97.	Mobile, Alabama	31,076
48.	Reading, Pennsylvania	58,661	98.	Topeka, Kansas	31,007
49.	Camden, New Jersey	58,313	99.	Elmira, New York	30,893
50.	Trenton, New Jersey	57,458	100.	Salem, Massachusetts	30,801

Source: U.S. Department of the Interior, Census Office, *Report on Population of the United States at the Eleventh Census: 1890*. Part I, pp. 370-372. Washington, D.C.: G.P.O.; 1895

100 Most Populous Cities In The United States: 1990

1.	New York, New York	7,322,564	51.	Wichita, Kansas	304,011
2.	Los Angeles, California	3,485,398	52.	Santa Ana, California	293,742
3.	Chicago, Illinois	2,783,726	53.	Mesa, Arizona	288,091
4.	Houston, Texas	1,630,553	54.	Colorado Springs, Colorado	281,140
5.	Philadelphia, Pennsylvania	1,585,577	55.	Tampa, Florida	280,015
6.	San Diego, California	1,110,549	56.	Newark, New Jersey	275,221
7.	Detroit, Michigan	1,027,974	57.	St. Paul, Minnesota	272,235
8.	Dallas, Texas	1,006,877	58.	Louisville, Kentucky	269,063
9.	Phoenix, Arizona	983,403	59.	Anaheim, California	266,406
10.	San Antonio, Texas	935,933	60.	Birmingham, Alabama	265,968
11.	San Jose, California	782,248	61.	Arlington, Texas	261,721
12.	Indianapolis, Indiana	741,952	62.	Norfolk, Virginia	261,229
13.	Baltimore, Maryland	736,014	63.	Las Vegas, Nevada	258,295
14.	San Francisco, California	723,959	64.	Corpus Christi, Texas	257,453
15.	Jacksonville, Florida	672,971	65.	St. Petersburg, Florida	238,629
16.	Columbus, Ohio	632,910	66.	Rochester, New York	231,636
17.	Milwaukee, Wisconsin	628,088	67.	Jersey City, New Jersey	228,537
18.	Memphis, Tennessee	610,337	68.	Riverside, California	226,505
19.	Washington, D.C.	606,900	69.	Anchorage, Alaska	226,338
20.	Boston, Massachusetts	574,283	70.	Lexington-Fayette, Kentucky	225,366
21.	Seattle, Washington	516,259	71.	Akron, Ohio	223,019
22.	El Paso, Texas	515,342	72.	Aurora, Colorado	222,103
23.	Nashville-Davidson, Ten.	510,784	73.	Baton Rouge, Louisiana	219,531
24.	Cleveland, Ohio	505,616	74.	Stockton, California	210,943
25.	New Orleans, Louisiana	496,938	75.	Raleigh, North Carolina	207,951
26.	Denver, Colorado	467,610	76.	Richmond, Virginia	203,056
27.	Austin, Texas	465,622	77.	Shreveport, Louisiana	198,525
28.	Fort Worth, Texas	447,619	78.	Jackson, Mississippi	196,637
29.	Oklahoma City, Oklahoma	444,719	79.	Mobile, Alabama	196,278
30.	Portland, Oregon	437,319	80.	Des Moines, Iowa	193,187
31.	Kansas City, Missouri	435,146	81.	Lincoln, Nebraska	191,262
32.	Long Beach, California	429,433	82.	Madison, Wisconsin	191,262
33.	Tucson, Arizona	405,390	83.	Grand Rapids, Michigan	189,126
34.	St. Louis, Missouri	396,685	84.	Yonkers, New York	188,082
35.	Charlotte, North Carolina	395,934	85.	Hialeah, Florida	188,004
36.	Atlanta, Georgia	394,017	86.	Montgomery, Alabama	187,106
37.	Virginia Beach, Virginia	393,069	87.	Lubbock, Texas	186,206
38.	Albuquerque, New Mexico	384,736	88.	Greensboro, North Carolina	183,521
39.	Oakland, California	372,242	89.	Dayton, Ohio	182,044
40.	Pittsburgh, Pennsylvania	369,879	90.	Huntington Beach, California	181,519
41.	Sacramento, California	369,365	91.	Garland, Texas	180,650
42.	Minneapolis, Minnesota	368,383	92.	Glendale, California	180,038
43.	Tulsa, Oklahoma	367,302	93.	Columbus, Georgia	179,278
44.	Honolulu, Hawaii	365,272	94.	Spokane, Washington	177,196
45.	Cincinnati, Ohio	364,040	95.	Tacoma, Washington	176,664
46.	Miami, Florida	358,548	96.	Little Rock, Arkansas	175,795
47.	Fresno, California	354,202	97.	Bakersfield, California	174,820
48.	Omaha, Nebraska	335,795	98.	Fremont, California	173,339
49.	Toledo, Ohio	332,943	99.	Fort Wayne, Indiana	173,072
50.	Buffalo, New York	328,123	100.	Newport News, Virginia	170,045

Source: U.S. Department of Commerce, Bureau of the Census, *Final Report: Population of U.S. Cities, Twenty-First Census, 1990.* Reprinted in: *World Almanac and Book of Facts, 1992.* New York: Scripps Howard; 1991.

Index

Illustrations are indicated by italics.

Dave Walter, research director of the Montana Historical Society, Helena, also is the author of Christmastime in Montana (1990), *and contributes a history column to* Montana Magazine.